Goodies From the Great White North

A cooking memoir

Leigh Goodison

Goodies from the Great White North

Reproduction or utilization of this work in any form, by any means now known or hereinafter invented, including, but not limited to, xerography, photocopying and recording, podcasting, and in any known storage and retrieval system, is forbidden without permission from the copyright holder.

SHEFFIELD PUBLICATIONS
www.sheffieldpublications.com

Copyright © 2012 Leigh Goodison

Cover design © Meghan Grieve

The text for this book is set in Arial.

Printed and bound in the United States of America.

10 9 8 7 6 5 4 3

Goodies from the Great White North / Leigh Goodison/ 2nd Edition

Summary:

A cooking memoir with over seventy recipes.

[1. Cooking/ Regional & Ethnic / Canadian

2. Cooking / Regional & Ethnic / International]

All rights reserved.

ISBN-13: 9781945136207
ISBN-10: 1-945136-20-0

Goodies From the Great White North

A cooking memoir

Leigh Goodison

Leigh Goodison

DEDICATION

This cooking memoir is dedicated to my mother and father,
Mary and Harold Goodison, and my children,
Meghan and James Grieve. Without them I would not have
perfected my culinary skills or survived the cooking catastrophes.

Goodies From the Great White North

CONTENTS

	Introduction	Pg 1
1	This Pie is the Pits	Pg 3
2	Drunken Dogs	Pg 17
3	Accept No Substitutes	Pg 23
4	Bachelor Daze	Pg 31
5	An Offal Thanksgiving	Pg 39
6	Fire Over Britain	Pg 51
7	What Boob Made This Cake?	Pg 67
8	Of Men and Machines	Pg 81
9	Into the Mouths of Babes	Pg 95
10	Rodent Flambé	Pg 101
11	What a Treat	Pg 107
12	Just a Hunka Hunka Burning Toast	Pg 111
13	Mom and Macs	Pg 113
	Index to Recipes	Pg 118

Goodies From the Great White North

INTRODUCTION

Growing up in a primarily English family in Canada, I struggled with a cultural identity crisis: was I English first, Canadian second? My friends and neighbors were all from 'somewhere else' and had their own ethnic backgrounds. With that heritage came recipes handed down from their parents' homeland. Ultimately, the melting pot of cultures that is North America influenced my cooking. What I came to think of Canadian recipes were those adapted and blended between my own and the multitudes of other cultures I was exposed to over the years.

My mother's side had a long line of good cooks and bakers. My father's side of the family was English and no one ever has anything good to say about English cooks. Can you imagine someone asking for the recipe for steak and kidney pie? Bangers and mash? Mushy peas?

Canadian recipes turn out best when authentic Canadian ingredients are used, such as Roger's Golden Syrup and Robin Hood or Five Roses Flour, but there are good substitutes for these. Like other people, I've been asked for many of my recipes and have my 'tried and trues.' It's usually when I experiment, or substitute, or try something different, that I come to grief. Most people will groan and say, "We'll laugh at that later." That's why I have included my recipe disasters. If you can't laugh at yourself, who else can you laugh at?

Leigh Goodison

THIS PIE IS THE PITS

My earliest memory of my father is visiting him at the Shaughnessy Hospital in Vancouver, British Columbia after he received a medical discharge from the Canadian Army. At that time the Shaughnessy was used primarily as a veterans' hospital. Dad had been in the RCEME Corps of Mechanics and Engineers and had fought in both World War II and the Korean War. After enlisting at the age of 22, he had been stationed in North Africa, Japan, Sicily, Italy, Germany, Korea and God knows where else. His body was full of shrapnel and he suffered from recurring bouts of malaria that he'd picked up while stationed in North Africa.

I was about five at that time, my sister Vicky was three and my baby brother, Wayne was two. I loved to visit Dad in the hospital because, like the other soldiers, he received a large allotment of high quality, army-issue chocolate bars, and he would give most of them to us kids. The army was kind enough to also issue the all-you-could-smoke cigarettes, which would do what two wars had not been able to, and eventually kill him 24 years later.

Two years after Dad was discharged from hospital was an especially desolate time for my sister and me. We lost Wayne to kidney disease, and the family had the quiet emptiness that comes with the loss of a child. Medical insurance was not available to us in those days. To pay the exorbitant hospital and doctor bills, my parents were forced to sell off all the furniture except for our beds and the table and chairs. We bought an enormous tent, which seemed as large as a circus tent to us kids, and put it on my grandparents' property in East Kelowna.

The tent was pitched at the top of a hill, with no shade trees around for acres. That summer the thermometer on the shady side of the tent reached 117 degrees, and stayed nearly that hot all week. As was typical after a few days of very hot weather in the Okanagan Valley, we would have an intense electrical storm, which is rather intimidating when you're in a tent with metal poles. To this day the smell of wet canvas brings back memories of that summer.

Living in a tent with regular household furniture was rather surreal. Dad built a wooden porch on the front and screened it in because of the blistering heat during the daytime summer months, then numbingly cold in the evening. The breeze passing through the tent screen cooled it off and also kept out the mosquitoes and gnats. A wood-burning stove was installed in that porch to help heat the tent. We had a regular table and chairs in there and called it our Summer Kitchen, which sounded rather grand to me. I'm sure there was absolutely nothing in any of those living arrangements that would conform to modern day building codes. But we actually spent a winter in the tent while Dad worked on our permanent wood structure house we would eventually move into.

As we didn't have electricity, our lighting consisted of coal oil lamps, which would smoke and flicker something awful when the wick got short. When the wick was too long, the chimney of the lamp became blackened. We had just about everything people in regular houses had except for a refrigerator. In the old days it was quite a trick to keep things cool and fresh. But our alternative was a root cellar, an underground cave with wood supports and shelves built into the dirt walls, a system people have been using for hundreds of years.

Every year Mom grew a spectacular garden, even though we had to haul water up to that dry, barren hill. What she couldn't grow we bought, mostly fruit like cherries, peaches, pears and apricots. In the heart of the fruit growing capital of Canada there was no shortage in variety or quantity. She diligently preserved everything she could so we would enjoy it during the winter months. It would be an understatement to say there was no money. In the economic climate after the Korean War, my father, who'd had a medical discharge from serving in two wars with the Canadian Army, had been out of work for some time. Mom's canning guaranteed we always had something to eat.

At that time, my sister and I were still unschooled as to the intricacies of canning fruit and vegetables. I was terrified of the pressure cooker, which once blew its top when the steam pressure failed to vent properly. Mom usually did the canning on a wood stove outside, for good reason, because the explosion could have killed or severely injured us. I remember her disappointment at not only the loss of the valuable Mason jars, but the beans we'd worked so hard to raise, pick, clean and chop. Now they were sprayed all over the outside of the tent like dull green insulation.

I left the mysterious canning process to my mother, who was fearless in that department. The only thing that fascinated me about canned food was that mysterious 'pop' we were told to watch for when we removed the lid from the sealed jars. There was always a fight to be the one to remove the lid because it was a 'one-time-deal' only. One 'pop' per sealed jar. We'd been warned many times that if it didn't 'pop', under no circumstances were we to eat whatever was in there.

In the cooking area, my father had a number of strikes against him. He was male, he was English, and he had grown up in the times when most men, other than professional chefs, didn't cook. So when Mom had to be away from the house for any length of time and Dad had to cook, it was anyone's guess as to what we would be eating.

My father was the most well-read person I have ever known, and had a whimsical sense of humor. Although he could barely open a can of food and reheat it without disaster, he devised a method to get us kids to eat by renaming otherwise inedible dishes to make them intriguing. And he didn't do it in a way that mothers would, like naming food 'Princess Peas' or 'Duchess Mashed Potatoes.' His unidentifiable creations were called things like 'schplat', 'glup' and 'schploot,' which suited them well.

I was eight years old when my mother went in to the hospital to give birth to my brother Bobby. I remember feeling very lost and lonely; suddenly it was just my sister and me with my dad. It had been less than a year since Wayne had died and the household was still quiet and sad. But not only that, now Dad would have to cook for us. Then suddenly Uncle Pete, my mother's brother, announced that he and his family were coming up from Vancouver for a visit to 'help us out.'

My mother wasn't overjoyed with this idea. She had a large, flourishing garden and she feared it would be pillaged while she was gone. In addition, and even worse for us girls, Aunt Margaret, who was English like my father, was a horrible cook.

However, we really liked Uncle Pete, who was a goofy kind of funny like my mother. And Aunt Margaret was the sweetest person we'd ever met. Our two cousins, Valerie and Marie, were very close to our own age, and although they were a little shy, we enjoyed their company. So, we decided to make the best of it and look forward to their visit.

Poor Aunt Margaret! There was nothing she could make that appealed to us girls. Her own daughters seemed to like it fine, but they were very sickly, pale, and unbelievably skinny, as was Uncle Pete. And although we were very hungry, we just couldn't bring ourselves to eat some of her concoctions. So we decided to just eat raw vegetables out of Mom's garden. We ate an awful lot of uncooked peas, carrots and corn.

But then Aunt Margaret offered to bake a cherry pie. This seemed like something we could fill up on and so we waited in anticipation for it to come out of the oven. It smelled wonderful and for an English cook the crust looked quite tasty. We all sat down and waited for her to slice a piece for us.

As host and head of the household, Dad was the first to get his. But even though the piece looked innocent enough, Vicky and I knew enough to wait until someone else ate first. There was silence around the table as Dad put the first forkful of pie into his mouth.

Suddenly there was an ominous 'crack!'

"Ow!" yelped Dad, in obvious pain. Daintily he removed the offending item from his mouth. It was a cherry pit. I looked down at my pie. It was filled with cherry pits.

Aunt Margaret had used Mom's cherry preserves to make the pie, but hadn't stopped to check and see if they'd been pitted. They hadn't. Those of us who were hungry enough were able to remove some of the cherry pits and eat the pie anyhow. Dad couldn't. As it turned out, he had broken his dentures in half and wasn't able to use them until he got new ones a week later. So he spent the entire visit with Uncle Pete, Aunt Margaret and the girls sounding like a little old man without his teeth.

Perfect Pastry

2 1/2 cups flour
3/4 tsp salt
1/4 lb butter (very cold)
1/3 cup vegetable shortening

Ice cold water**

Combine 2 1/2 cups of the flour and 3/4 tsp salt. Cut in 1/4 lb of the butter and the shortening until the mixture resembles coarse meal.

Toss in as much cold water as needed, a couple of tablespoons at a time, until the ingredients begin to clump together. Press into a ball, wrap and refrigerate. Don't over work the dough when rolling out. Try and roll only one time as each time you rework the dough you'll blend the butter in more.

**The secret to perfect crust is that the ingredients need to be very cold so the butter and shortening is in pea-sized chunks, not blended in. This is what makes the pastry flakey. Take a measuring cup, half fill it with ice, then fill it to the top with water. This pie pastry is excellent for meat pies because the baked product has a bistro texture.

If you are making a dessert pie, reduce the butter by two tbsp and increase the shortening by two tbsp. More shortening makes the crust more crumbly (called 'short'); more butter makes the crust more pliable and hold together better for heavy contents.

Apple Pie

6 cups sliced applies (7-8, MacIntosh or Granny Smith)
1/2 cup sugar (3/4 if using tart applies like Granny Smith)
2 tbsp flour
1 tbsp butter
1/2 cinnamon

Perfect Pastry

1 egg, beaten
1 tbsp water

Prepare pie crust and chill while preparing the filling.

Heat oven to 425 F. Peel and core the apples. Slice into 1/4" slices. Mix the dry ingredients together, then gently toss into the apples. Roll pie crust out to make a top and bottom crust, place the apples over the bottom crust. Dot with 1 tbsp butter, then place top crust over apples and pinch to seal edges. Prick holes or a design into top crust, then glaze with a wash of 1 egg beaten with 1 tbsp water.

Bake for 15 minutes at 425 F, glaze pie with egg mixture again, then lower oven to 350 F and bake for approximately 35 minutes. If pie begins to get too brown, cover with a layer of aluminum foil, shiny side down.

Blueberry Pie

4 cups fresh or frozen blueberries
3/4 cup sugar
4 tbsp cornstarch
3/4 tsp cinnamon
2 tbsp melted butter
1 tbsp lemon juice

Perfect Pastry

Place bottom crust in pie plate. Mix all ingredients together then place fruit mixture into bottom crust. Cover with top crust and pinch to seal edges. Prick holes or a design into top crust, then glaze with a wash of 1 egg beaten with 1 tbsp water.

Bake for 15 minutes at 425 F, glaze pie with egg mixture again, then lower oven to 350 F and bake for approximately 70 minutes. If pie begins to get too brown, cover with a layer of aluminum foil, shiny side down.

Butter Tarts

1/2 cup butter
1 cup brown sugar
3 eggs, beaten
2 cups raisins
1 tsp vanilla

Perfect Pastry

Melt butter on low heat, stir in sugar and eggs. Add raisins. Bring to a bubbling boil then immediately turn off heat. Add vanilla. Stir and let cool. Roll out pastry and cut into 4" circles. Place dough in muffin tins and then fill dough with filling, nearly to the top. Bake at 375 F for 10-12 minutes.

Daiquiri Pie

4 egg whites
1 envelope unflavored gelatin
4 egg yolks
1/2 cup lime juice
1/4 cup rum (or water)
1 cup sugar, separated
1/4 tsp salt
1 tbsp grated lime rind
Green food coloring
1 cup heavy cream, separated
9 inch baked pie shell

In large bowl, let egg whites warm to room temperature for 1 hour.

Sprinkle gelatin over rum (or water) in small bowl. Let gelatin stand 5 minutes to soften.

In top of double boiler, beat egg yolks slightly. Beat in lime juice, 1/2 cup sugar, and salt. Cook over hot, not boiling, water, stirring until mixture thickens slightly and coats the spoon. Remove from heat. Add gelatin and lime peel, stirring until gelatin is dissolved. Add 2 drops of food coloring, mix well. Set mixture aside to cool.

At high speed beat egg whites just until soft peaks form when beater is raised. Gradually beat in remaining 1/2 cup sugar, 2 tbsp at a time, beating well after each addition. Continue beating until stiff peaks form when beater is raised.

Whip 1/2 cup cream until stiff. With rubber scraper or wire whisk, gently fold gelatin mixture and whipped cream into egg white mixture until just combined. (Continued on Page 20)

Daiquiri Pie
(Continued from Page 19)

Turn into pie shell, mounting high. Refrigerate until firm, several hours or overnight. Whip rest of cream until stiff. Garnish pie with dabs of whipped cream, or use a pastry bag to create a fancy design.

Grasshopper Pie

1/4 cup butter
1 tbsp plus 3/4 cup sugar
26 chocolate wafers, crushed (about 1 1/2 cups)
1 envelope unflavored gelatin
1 package softened cream cheese
1/2 cup water
1/3 cup green crème de menthe
2 cups heavy whipping cream

Melt butter in small saucepan, stir in the 1 tbsp sugar and the crumbs. Press 2/3 cup of the crumbs in the bottom of an 8" pie pan. Chill while preparing the filling.

Sprinkle gelatin over water in small saucepan, let stand 5 minutes to soften. Stir over very low heat until gelatin is dissolved.

Beat cream cheese with remaining 3/4 cup sugar in small bowl with electric mixer until fluffy. Gradually beat in gelatin mixture. Stir in crème de menthe.

Reserve 1/2 cup whipped cream for garnish, fold remainder into cream cheese mixture.

Pour half of the filling into the crumb lined pan, reserve 2 tbsp crumbs for garnish, and top evenly with remaining crumbs. Pour in remaining filling. Garnish with reserved crumbs and whipped cream. Chill until set, about 4 hours.

Strawberry Pie

1 cup crushed strawberries
2 cups whole strawberries
2 1/2 tbsp cornstarch
1/2 cup cold water
1 cup sugar
1/8 tsp salt
1 tbsp lemon juice

9" baked pie shell

Combine sugar, salt and cornstarch. Add water and crushed berries. Mix well. Cook until thick and clear, stirring constantly. Add lemon juice. Cool. Spread half of the glaze in bottom of baked pie shell. Add whole berries. Spread remaining glaze on top. Chill. Serve with whipped cream or ice cream.

Toy Chow Pie (China)

1 cup chow mein noodles
3 egg whites
3 tsp cream of tartar
1 cup sugar
2 tsp vanilla
1/2 cup lemon extract
1 cup chopped walnuts
2 small boxes frozen strawberries (2 cups fresh sliced strawberries or other berries can be used)

1 cup whipping cream

2 tsp powdered sugar

Crush noodles, beat egg whites and cream of tartar until stiff. Gradually add sugar and continue beating until stiff. Fold in 1 tsp vanilla, lemon extract, noodles and walnuts. Spread meringue into a well-buttered 9" pie plate. Mound to sides, leaving bottom slightly hollow for filling. Bake at 325 F for 35 minutes. Remove from heat. Cool completely. Cut into 8 servings. Place on dessert plates. Top with partially thawed strawberries. Whip the cream and the powdered sugar. Add remaining 1 tsp vanilla. Top strawberries with whipped cream, garnish with a few chow mein noodles.

Mocha Devil's Food Cake

1/2 cup cocoa
1 tbsp instant coffee
2/3 cup boiling water
1/2 cup buttermilk**
2/3 cup shortening
1 1/2 cups sugar
3 eggs
2 cups flour
1 1/2 tsp baking soda
1/2 tsp salt

Preheat oven to 350 F. Grease and lightly flour 2 9" layer pans. Combine cocoa and instant coffee in a small bowl. Blend in boiling water and cool to lukewarm. Stir in buttermilk. Cream shortening and sugar. Beat in eggs, one at a time, until mixture is light and fluffy. Sift dry ingredients and fold into creamed mixture alternately with cocoa liquid. Spread batter in prepared pans. Bake 30 – 35 minutes. When cool, frost as desired, or sprinkle with powdered sugar.

**As I rarely have buttermilk available, I substitute 1 tsp of white vinegar added to 1/2 cup of whole milk.

DRUNKEN DOGS

If there's one thing I've learned over the years, it's that dogs will eat *anything*. Oh, not all dogs will eat everything; some won't touch vegetables, while others love them. Some will turn up their noses at the most choice commercial dog food, yet scavenge scraps from garbage cans. There's no point whatsoever in using dogs as taste-testers in meal preparation as they have no discriminating palate. An offering will either be gobbled down immediately, or sniffed at as suspiciously as if it were poisoned.

Unfortunately, many of us use our beloved pets as walking garbage cans. We can't bear to throw away those leftovers: *We* won't eat them, so we toss them to poor Fido. Let him be the one to gain the pounds or get a queasy stomach from that past-due ham.

So far in my life I've been lucky enough to have enjoyed five family dogs. And though my memory may have diminished over the years, it seems as though I've loved each dog better than the last. Definitely, some have been more loyal than others and the term 'man's best friend' can sometimes be a generous term for what are more often self-serving animals.

For instance, I once witnessed our beloved dog B-fer, gently and methodically slip a chocolate bar from the hands of my diabetic, semi-conscious husband; something I had given him to raise his blood sugar. She slipped off to savor the treat herself, never mind that chocolate is considered deadly to dogs. A fact they are seemingly unaware of as most dogs I know crave chocolate as much as I do.

Despite her chocolate feast, B-fer lived to be thirteen, a ripe old age for large dogs. The loss of every pet is gut-wrenching agony to me. It was only a couple of weeks after her passing that I began scouring the newspaper for puppies. I had quite a few necessary requirements in a dog: they had to be large, good watchdog material, and they must not shed. Oh, and they had to smell relatively good. Of course that narrowed the list down considerably.

Gary and I eventually came to the agreement that we would get a half-bred or mutt, rather than a purebred dog. We lived on a small river front acreage, but I didn't want a water dog. Nearly all the mutt puppies I found were a Labrador crossed with something else. These did not appeal to me at all.

Then one day I saw an ad for Great Pyrenees/German Shepherd puppies. Intrigued, we dashed out to see them, knowing full well that if you go out to look at puppies, you're pretty much guaranteed to be coming home with one. In fact, it was a difficult task to choose just one of the litter of five.

We arrived in time to have the pick of the litter. Because I had chosen our last dog, and my family seemed impressed with my ability to pick a good one, I had creative control again. I chose the largest, most aggressive female. We named her Xena, Warrior Princess.

We had taken an empty beer carton, lined with a towel, to pick up the puppy. But as we squeezed the six-week-old puppy into it, we realized we were going to end up with a fairly large dog.

When Xena was about three months old, my son's fraternity had a 'rush party' at our house. My ex husband and I stayed discreetly in the basement watching television. We had given strict instructions that there were to be no underage drinkers, and trusted the older, more responsible organizers of the frat.

It was a relatively quiet party, considering the group, but before too long I began to wonder where the puppy was. I hadn't seen her in several hours, mostly because the young people upstairs had been playing fetch with her. I went upstairs to the sundeck to find most of the guests had gone, with just a couple of people left playing cards. The puppy was asleep in a lawn chair.

I picked her up and carried her downstairs with me. She stayed sleeping, her legs dangling as limply as a Beanie Baby dog's. I laid her carefully on the sofa beside Gary, then sat down to watch television.

After the program was over, I said, "Did you ever see a puppy sleep so soundly?"

He glanced over at her. "The kids must have really played her out," he said. "She's out cold."

Suddenly I got suspicious. I went over and tried to wake her. She opened her eyes slowly, then closed them again and fell asleep. I picked her up, legs dangling, and set her on the floor. She took a few unsteady steps forward, then tipped over and fell asleep again.

I looked at Gary and we both realized what must have happened. I ran upstairs, ready to tear a strip off of whoever it was who had given the dog beer. But by the time I'd finished yelling, no one was interested in confessing. The most I got out of anyone was, "Well, she didn't turn it down." Which was what most underage drinkers would have done, I suppose.

When I was about eight years old, we got our first family dog. We called him the original name of "Boots" because of his white socks. An unneutered black and white collie/lab cross with an uneven temper, he was the least of our favorites. But like all dogs he had his endearing moments.

Boots was not much of a playmate. He was more of a 'run-off-to-neighboring-acreages-to-see-what-females-were-around' type of dog. He didn't fetch, he didn't play any kind of ball or dog/kid type things with us. Still, we'd invite him to go off with us when we played.

One evening for dessert, my mother opened a jar of preserved cherries and the lid didn't make the required 'pop'. There was an ominous silence around the table. Mom didn't say a word, she just took the jar outside to dump on the compost heap later.

After dinner, my sister and I went out to play. One of my favorite games was to disrupt the dozens of enormous ant hills that dotted the plateau on which we lived. I never tired of flattening the ant hills until the eggs were exposed, then watched as the ants scurried to rebuild and move their precious eggs. I used to dream up ant newspaper headlines, stories teaming with death and destruction.

But soon we were bored with annihilating ants that have no interaction at all. So we called Boots to come and play. But that day, Boots was nowhere to be seen. Vicky and I set off to look for him.

Mom was just finishing the dinner dishes and scraping the table scraps into Boot's dish when we walked up. She hadn't seen him either. Then we rounded the corner of the tent and to witness the most amazing sight. Boots was bounding into the air, performing the most death-defying leaps as he skipped across the yard. To this day, I swear he kicked his hind heels as he bounced.

I looked at my sister and we both started to laugh. But then we got serious. We'd just seen the Disney movie *Old Yeller*, and we knew about hydrophobia. Maybe Boots had hydrophobia. We ran to get Mom. But Mom was just as perplexed as us girls. She had a hard time suppressing a smile, but went to fetch Dad. Dad knew more about dogs than anyone. And Boots was the offspring of his parents' dogs. When Dad saw Boots he started to laugh, too.

"He's drunk," said Dad. He turned and walked away as if this was something all dogs do when not busy being watchdogs and playmates.

But this was a new one to us kids. We were not familiar with alcohol as no one in our family drank. Where would the dog have gotten liquor?

"Maybe from a Boots-legger," my sister volunteered helpfully, apparently knowing more than I did on the subject.

But Boots continued to dance erratically around the yard. Mom was starting to get concerned.

"I think there's something wrong with him," she said. "If he keeps acting this way, Dad will have to do something."

We cringed. In those days animal owners had to make difficult life and death decisions and implement them without veterinary assistance. 'Do something' meant taking him out and putting him out of his misery (or happiness). But as we continued to watch, Boots started to slow down. Within minutes he'd crawled into his dog house to sleep it off.

Party Punch (with a punch)

26 oz vodka
26 oz sparkling rosé wine
One large 48 oz can of fruit punch
2 liters of 7-Up
Fresh strawberries and orange slices

Mix all together except for the fruit. Chill. Serve in a large punch bowl with freshly sliced fruit.

Hot Canadian Toddy (whoever Tod is)

2 tbsp Roger's Golden Syrup (or pure maple syrup)
1 shot rum
Boiling water
1 tsp butter
Cinnamon

Put Roger's Golden Syrup and rum in bottom of mug. Fill to top with boiling water. Stir. Float butter on top and sprinkle with cinnamon. One serving.

Gluhwein

(spiced hot wine, pronounced Gloo-vine)

2 bottles Burgundy wine
8 slices lemon
8 slices orange
6 sticks cinnamon
6 cloves
1 cup sugar

Mix all together in a large, non-metallic saucepan. Heat to almost boiling then turn down to a gentle simmer. Serve hot. Great for post ski parties!

ACCEPT NO SUBSTITUTES

In my early cooking years I truly believed in the old adage, 'The way to a man's heart is through his stomach.' My first boyfriend was pampered, the youngest child of the family. His mother cooked, cleaned and pretty much did everything mothers were supposed to do back in the fifties and sixties. I took over where she left off and tried to impress him with my cooking and baking abilities. Unfortunately, the only recipe book I owned at the time was a Campbell's *Cooking With Soup* book, so my range was limited.

In high school I'd taken cooking classes, and developed a real knack for breads, cookies and cakes. But I never really had much experience in the meal department. When I moved away from home to go to college I had a minimally stocked kitchen and found myself substituting a lot of items. My substitutes were fairly random. For instance, if a recipe called for cardamom and all I had was cinnamon, it sounded close enough. Curry powder was substituted for cumin, tarragon for turmeric, etc. Actually, as it turned out, most of these worked fairly well. Years later when my kitchen became better stocked and I tried the same recipes with the correct ingredients, I found I didn't like them as well as I had with the substitutes. Go figure.

I was about to embark on the first real home-cooked meal for my boyfriend. He lived in another town and had called to say he'd be in around dinner-time. I lived in a motel that became student housing during off-season. Because I was a student, my limited budget didn't allow for a lot of groceries to keep on hand. I spent hours poring over cook books, trying to figure out what kind of 'man-pleasing' recipe I could make with what I had. Then I found a recipe for *coq au vin* (chicken with wine), a dish I'd been as fascinated by as *crepes suzette*, and one I'd always wanted to try. There was just one problem. More than one, as it turned out.

I glanced through the freezer and discovered the only meat I had was stewing beef. There was no time left to go to the market and besides, I didn't have any money. Therefore, it would be *boeuf au vin*. I consulted the cook book. Now I needed wine. Dry, white wine. I went to the cupboard. I had wine. But it was a sparkling rosé, a Canadian fermentation called 'Fuddle Duck,' a parody of Cold Duck sparkling rosé. It had gotten the name Fuddle Duck due to a remark made by the late Canadian Prime Minister, Pierre Trudeau when asked to explain unemployment and inflation. His comment was 'fuddle-duddle.' Kind of the Canadian equivalent of 'Let them eat cake." Don't ask me why someone went the step further and named a bad wine after that but they obviously thought it had some market value. *I* bought it, so it must have worked.

Fuddle Duck it would have to be, although my experience in cooking with alcohol was limited. Non-existent actually, as my parents had never allowed alcohol in the house. Even if they had, they certainly wouldn't have used it for cooking other than fuel for a Sterno-oven.

I measured out the correct amount of wine, noting glumly how it sparkled and fizzed as I poured it into the cup. And although it wasn't white, it wasn't *red*, either, sort of pinkish. Close enough to white. I had enough sense to let it sit at room temperature for awhile so it would go flat like real cooking wine.

In spite of the wine substitution, I followed the rest of the recipe closely and after browning the meat, added the wine and the spices. Then I let it simmer the required two hours and crossed my fingers. It didn't smell very good, but I thought simmering it might help tenderize the tough stewing beef and bring all the flavors together. I was wrong. The flavors came together all right, but not in a *good* way. And it certainly wasn't the flavor I was after.

Although my boyfriend was due to arrive any time, I knew I couldn't serve that mess. It tasted abominable. I also couldn't place it in the inside garbage because it stunk something awful and if he saw it he would know I was a failure as a cook. I couldn't put in the outdoor garbage bin because it would attract the host of stray cats that frequented the garbage. The landlord had warned us not to feed them, and he had an uncanny way of tracing garbage back to the original owner. The best thing to do would be to flush the whole mess down the toilet. Which I did.

As a substitute meal, I got out a spaghetti sauce spice packet and prepared a quick batch of 'homemade' sauce. This impromptu back-up meal turned out to be acceptable entertainment fare as we had a salad, garlic bread and the last of the Fuddle Duck to wash it down. After the meal, I started to clean up the kitchen and my boyfriend went to use the bathroom. He rushed out several minutes later.

"Do you have a plunger?" he said. "Your toilet's plugged."

A strange sense of foreboding came over me. I handed him the plunger. After a few minutes he came out again, looking concerned.

"It's not working," he said, "there's water all over the floor. We'd better get the landlord."

My heart sank. My landlord was a spoiled, lazy rich 'kid' in his late '20's, whose parents had bought him the motel (I rented one unit) to keep him busy when it became apparent he'd never use the law degree he'd earned in college. I wasn't afraid that he'd be angry at the mess in the bathroom, but if he saw the wine and perceived that there was any kind of a party going on, he'd crash it and I'd never get rid of him. And his endless collection of Spencer Davis records. Then I saw the water seeping out the bathroom door. What choice did I have?

The landlord came over with his 'snake,' a device which coiled down into the depths of the plumbing and was designed to unplug the most stubborn of toilets. I remembered from a previous encounter that his snake was a precious and much revered tool. I chose to stay in the kitchen and not watch. I could hear the landlord swearing and panting in the bathroom for what seemed like an eternity. After about twenty minutes or so, the landlord came out, sweating and filthy.

"That was really plugged," he said. "What the hell did you have down there?"

I remained mute so as to not incriminate myself.

"Something really plugged it," he said, fishing.

There was no way I would admit to what I'd done. "Nothing any different than usual," I said, finding the conversation unbelievably embarrassing.

He shook his head, the water dripping off his 'snake' as he walked across the kitchen floor.

"I can't figure it out," he said as he paused at the door, looking back toward the bathroom reflectively, "if I didn't know better, I'd swear that was meat in there."

Hot Cabbage Salad

1/2 cup celery
1 1/2 cup cabbage
1/3 cup olive oil (or Italian salad dressing)
1 tbsp chopped onion
Salt & pepper to taste

Heat oil, add cabbage, celery, salt and pepper. Cook until tender, about 8 minutes. Drain off oil, serve hot.

Ambrosia Salad

1 cup sour cream (small carton)
1 cup coconut
1 small can mandarin orange slices, drained
1 can pineapple chunks (or 1 can crushed, drained pineapple)
1 cup miniature marshmallows

Mix all ingredients and refrigerate overnight or several hours before serving. Fruit cocktail in the same quantities can be substituted for the pineapple and oranges.

Asian Rice Salad

1 cup long grain rice
1 10 oz can sliced mushrooms, drained
1/2 cup olive oil
1/4 cup cider vinegar
2 tbsp soy sauce
1/2 tsp salt
1 10 oz can mandarin orange segments, drained
1 cup thinly sliced celery
2 tbsp thinly sliced green onions
1/2 cup slivered almonds
Lettuce

Cook rice by bringing 2 cups of water and 1 tsp salt to the boil, add rice, stir with fork, cover and reduce to a simmer for 25 minutes until all the water is absorbed. Cool.

While rice is cooking combine, oil, vinegar, soy sauce and salt in a jar with a lid and shake to combine. Add mushrooms to the cooled rice, and pour the oil mixture over. Toss rice and mushrooms lightly, cover and chill at least an hour. Just before serving fold in mandarin oranges, celery, green onions and almonds. Spoon salad into lettuce lined bowl, or individual bowls. Garnish with additional oranges and slivered almonds.

Crazy Quilt Salad

1/3 can cut green beans
1/3 can cut wax beans
1/3 can red kidney beans
1/3 can Lima beans
1/4 cup chopped celery
2 tbsp onion rings or chunks
2 tbsp green pepper

Dressing

2 tbsp vinegar
1/4 cup salad oil
Pinch ground pepper
1/4 tsp dry mustard
1/4 tsp thyme
1/8 tsp salt
Pinch garlic salt

Pour dressing over vegetables in a container with a tight seal. Let stand overnight. Turn upside down to marinate. Note: if you wish to use the entire cans of beans above, increase the other ingredients by 2/3 more (i.e., using the entire can of beans). This will make a large amount, suitable for entertaining.

Western Sandwiches

3 eggs
3 tbsp water
2 tbsp finely chopped green pepper
1/2 cup finely chopped ham
2 tbsp finely chopped onion
1 tsp salt
1/2 tsp pepper
1 tbsp butter
4 slices toast

Beat eggs with water, add salt and pepper, then the rest of the ingredients. Melt butter in 9" nonstick frying pan, add eggs, cooking on low to medium heat without stirring. Lift the edges of the omelet to let the uncooked eggs run underneath and cook, being careful not to let the underside get too brown. When the top side appears dry, flip it over and cook until egg is completely cooked. Place cooked egg mixture between toast slices and serve hot.

BACHELOR DAZE

There is an unbelievable sense of freedom when you first leave home. You are your own boss. No one can tell you to clean your room, do the dishes or pick up after yourself. You can let the laundry go for weeks until you need something to wear, the dishes can pile up, and until the landlord complains, you can forget to take out the garbage. It's sheer Heaven. That is, it's Heaven until alien life forms begin to grow in your apartment.

As a single woman I had not only been witness to some of the most abhorrent living conditions ever occupied by bachelors, but am ashamed to say that I have on occasion lived that way myself. The filth and degradation that singles will endure rivals the atrocious conditions of poverty-stricken people in war-torn, third world countries. In fact, there should be a special branch of Unicef or the Red Cross that provides aid directly to young people who have recently left the security and cleanliness of their parents' home.

It's difficult to know where the degradation first begins. It seems as if you have just bought that chip dip when suddenly free-form sculptures of fuzzy, green mold is lifting the lid. Buying fresh fruit or vegetables is pointless as you'll probably never get around to eating them and they only last a few days. Forget about them for a month and you'll never be able to identify the original food.

I remember making myself a gin and tonic one evening and rejoicing to find a lime in the bottom of my crisper. However, when I picked it up, the green came off on my fingers and I discovered that what I actually had was a lemon, now moldy and covered with fuzzy green flocking. I started buying packaged lime juice after that. But if *my* apartment was a state of disgrace, it was a mere runner-up in the male Olympics of Repugnance.

It's my opinion that young bachelors are the most disgusting creatures on earth. Until a woman enters their lives, it doesn't matter that every dish or pan they own is caked in food from a meal long past. But I would offer a word of advice to those men who are thinking of entertaining a female in their home: Move first!

My first visit to a 'bachelor pad' came shortly after I'd left college. My boyfriend had moved to another province and was living in an apartment with a couple of male roommates. After I'd moved in to my new place, he brought me to his apartment to meet his friends. When he opened the door, the smell almost knocked me over. He didn't seem to notice and headed to the bedrooms to find his roommates.

Coughing and gagging, I ventured gingerly into the kitchen, and what I saw there I'll never forget. The kitchen counters were stacked with dishes, pots and pans that were covered in dried food and flies of every size and species. Pizza boxes and other fast food packages were piled on top of those. It appeared that once they ran out of dishes they just started eating take-out food.

I don't know what possessed me to do this, but I was so revolted that I offered to help clean up. My boyfriend said they'd pay me if I did it. It was worth every cent to them. If a Health Inspector ever caught sight of the apartment, they'd never rent anywhere again.

I grabbed a large green garbage bag and began filling it with the debris in the kitchen. Soon I'd filled three bags and had finally gotten down to the pots and pans. And then the most amazing sight met my eyes. A saucepan on the counter that was filled with grey/green water was bubbling without benefit of heat. And oh, the smell!

I tied the cleanest tea towel I could find across my face and began scrubbing the pan with SOS pads. Eventually I had the saucepan and all the other dishes disinfected and put away. It still smelled like the city dump in there, but with a few windows open to get a cross breeze, it was almost tolerable.

"What the heck was in that pot?" I asked my boyfriend after I'd sterilized myself.

"I think it was originally Kraft Dinner," he said, "but I'm not sure. It's been there quite a while."

Then there was the garbage under the sink to remove. I opened the cupboard door under the sink and a few insects, startled by the light, scuttled away before I could identify them. This was extremely nasty, as can only be imagined, but there was also a large quantity of flies. I soon discovered that they were also raising families. In the corners of the cupboards, fly maggots were crawling along like babies taking their first steps. Killing maggots was the guys' job. They bred 'em, they could kill 'em.

I don't know why it is, but food made by the Kraft Corporation seems to mutate in a more surreal fashion than any other packaged foods I've purchased. The potato chip dip I referred to earlier was made by Kraft, as is Kraft Dinner. While other food just goes rotten and dangerously inedible, Kraft products become the art deco of former food. If I had a stronger stomach, I might be tempted to experiment in this art form, but those days are long gone and my memory is too poor. The chances of my forgetting and inadvertently eating it or serving it to my family are now too great.

This is not casting aspersions on the Kraft Corporation: quite the contrary. I've discovered that I can safely use Kraft Dinner long after the suggested 'best before' date. It's sort of like posted speed limits on the highway. Skilled or professional drivers know that they can safely exceed the speed limit without fear of death, but regular drivers like myself are better off adhering to the warnings.

    Years later I was married with children and on a second generation of single living slobs. My daughter's boyfriend lived with two other fellows and after visiting their home she discovered what I learned at her age: buy them paper plates. My son moved into a fraternity and the only maggots that were allowed in the house were the first year live-in's who were not only the grunts that performed kitchen duty, they were quite literally called maggots.

Chicken Noodle Soup

Chicken Stock

1 roasted chicken carcass (leftovers are fine, skin and all)
1 tbsp whole peppercorns
2 bay leaves

Soup Ingredients

2 carrots, sliced thinly
1 small onion, chopped
2 cups dry noodles or macaroni
Salt and pepper to taste

Place chicken carcass in large pot, cover with water, add peppercorns and bay leaves. Simmer, covered, for two hours. Carefully remove carcass and set aside on plate to cool. Strain the chicken broth into a large clean pot. Discard the peppercorns, bay leaves and any loose bits of bones remaining. Remove chicken meat from chicken carcass and cut into 1/2" pieces. Set aside.

To the broth in pan, add carrots, onion and noodles. Cook until noodles and carrots are tender. Add chopped chicken. Add salt and pepper to taste.

Note: the broth can be made ahead and used in other recipes or frozen for later use, such as in Mulligatawny.

Mulligatawny (India)

2 tbsp butter
3 stalks celery, sliced
1 large potato, peeled and diced
2 large onions, chopped fine
4 cloves garlic, chopped fine
2 carrots, diced
4 tsp curry powder
1/4 tsp ground cloves
1/2 tsp ground ginger
1/2 tsp cayenne
1 to 2 tsp salt
1 tsp Malabar pepper (or coarse black pepper)
8 cups chicken or turkey broth
3 cups diced cooked chicken
3 cups cooked white rice
1 apple, peeled and grated
1 tbsp lemon juice
1 cup sour cream

Melt butter in a large pot, and sauté celery, potato, onion, garlic, carrot and seasonings for 5 minutes. Add broth and simmer 20 minutes. Add chicken, rice, grated apple and lemon juice. Just before serving add sour cream and reheat.

Gazpacho (Spain)

2 1/2 cups water
1 beef bouillon cube
2 chicken bouillon cubes
1 1/2 cups tomato juice
1/2 tsp salt
1/4 tsp pepper
1 tsp paprika
2 medium tomatoes, diced
1 medium cucumber, peeled and diced
1/4 cup chopped onion
1 medium green pepper, chopped

Combine water, beef and chicken bouillon cubes, tomato juice, salt, pepper and paprika. Blend well. Stir in vegetables. Refrigerate two hours or overnight to blend flavors. Makes approximately two quarts.

Baked Rum Bananas

2 ripe bananas
1/4 cup butter
1/2 cup brown sugar
1/4 cup rum

Melt butter in saucepan on low heat, add brown sugar and stir until sugar is dissolved. Stir in rum. Turn off heat. Spoon half of butter mixture into square glass baking pan. Slice bananas in half, length wise. Place on top of butter mixture in baking pan, then spoon the remaining butter mixture over top. Place in microwave and cook on high 30 seconds. Remove from heat and turn bananas over in pan, basting them with the butter mix. Microwave on high another 30 seconds. Remove from heat, place bananas in individual heat proof serving bowls and top with a scoop of ice cream. Spoon brown sugar sauce over ice cream. Serves 2.

AN OFFAL THANKSGIVING

The fact that Mankind survived for thousands of years before refrigeration was invented is testimony to our hardiness as a species. In earlier times, food was killed and eaten as it was needed. Immediately. Or yesterday. Later on, man (or more likely, woman) dried food for long-term storage, considerately knocking the maggots out of the desiccated meat before serving it to their family. However, only those whose stomachs had become hardened to salmonella, trichinosis, or e-coli bacteria survived long enough to produce a new generation of cooks.

In the post-war era, with stay-at-home mothers and homemakers preparing the meals, supermarkets did not bother to offer precut salad greens or have full-course meals ready to pop in the oven. That was something the homemaker was expected to do. Moms were happy enough that the fish had already been gutted or that the pin feathers were singed from the chicken.

My mother had prepared most of the meals when I lived at home, and as she was so adept in the kitchen, I avoided asking for tuition in simple meal preparation. I had vivid memories of some of her dishes, and on occasion, could recreate to a degree a few of our family favorites.

After college, I moved to an apartment and lived alone with my cat. I had little interest in cooking, and because of a lively social schedule seldom ate at home. But I always returned long enough to feed Morris, a large ginger Manx with a jacked-up rear end. He had the speed and acceleration of a NHRA drag racing, 'funny car,' which prompted my boyfriend to dub him "Morris, the racing cat."

When I first set up housekeeping on my own I cherished the convenience and novelty of TV dinners, fascinated by their teeny-weeny entrees and mini-desserts. It was rare that I cooked just for myself. But after a few months of living on my own I began making friends and was invited over for meals at their homes. As is only natural, I eventually felt the need to reciprocate.

When my first Thanksgiving alone rolled around, the tradition of a more formal meal was needed. A lot of my friends were from somewhere else and unable to get home for a family Thanksgiving. Without truly thinking it through, I offered to host it at my apartment. It seemed elementary enough to cook dinner for some friends, but I was totally unprepared for the hellacious bird that would invade my home.

One of the most important things a new cook needs to know is the quantity of meat required for the number of invited guests. I was having five people for dinner. When I was a kid I remembered hearing my mother grumbling about her oven being too small for that 'damned 26 pound turkey.' Well, we had been a family of five. Five people were invited to my dinner party. Twenty-six pounds sounded about right. So that's what I bought on Thanksgiving eve. What I forgot about was the weeks of turkey sandwiches, turkey tetrazzini and turkey *a la king* that followed our Thanksgivings.

When I got that bird home and placed it on my counter, I thought that it looked SO MUCH LARGER than the turkeys of my youth. Not only was it enormous--it was frozen solid. I left it out on the counter all night to defrost but by morning it was still as hard as the iceberg that sank the Titanic. I checked the cookbook and discovered that it needed to be cooked for a half-hour per pound. In those days no one had microwaves, let alone me in a rented apartment. The only way I could get that turkey partially thawed was to run it under hot water.

After running the water over it for a half-hour, I eventually got the skin soft enough to stick a meat thermometer into the breast about one-quarter of an inch. It wouldn't go any further and I was afraid of breaking off the thermometer and getting mercury into the turkey. Merky-turkey sounded dangerous.

The stuffing had been prepared earlier in the day, but as I got ready to stick it in the turkey I realized that the cavity was so frozen that I could only get two cups of it into the body. I stuffed as much of the remainder as I could under the flabby neck skin, stuck some skewers in and around 2:00 p.m. put it in the oven to roast.

When my friends came over just before dinner time, they took one look in the oven and suggested that the turkey needed at least another five hours before it would be safe to eat. We drank, ate other things, drank some more, and had a good time. Eventually near midnight it was time to carve the turkey, and though I was rather inebriated by this time, I carved it, more or less, by hacking it apart with the only knife I owned: a very dull paring knife.

What we ate seemed to have turned out fairly well, considering the unconventional cooking method. In those days, the thought of food poisoning was one of the furthest things from my mind. As I always used basic common sense in food handling, washing carefully before and after handling meat, I'm assuming no one got sick. At least, everyone showed up to work the next morning. But it was the leftovers that stayed on to haunt me.

Because we'd filled ourselves on other things, I was still left with approximately 24 pounds of cooked turkey the next morning. Most of the stuffing had been eaten, but as I scraped out whatever was left, I was astounded to find a small bag crammed behind the stuffing. I pulled it out, opened it and looked inside. There was a turkey neck and several unidentified brownish lumps. I concluded these were organs, like the liver, heart and whatever else makes a turkey tick. No one had told me that the butcher routinely stuffed these back into the cavity.

I gave the offal (isn't that the most appropriate term you've ever heard?) to Morris the cat, tore off the rest of the turkey meat and refrigerated it. I put the carcass in the refrigerator for later too, as I intended to make soup stock out of it. But after a week, with the turkey cadaver still taking up most of my refrigerator, I decided to discard it. The carcass was too large to fit in my tiny garbage can under the sink, and it was still several days before garbage pickup, so I set it out on the balcony of my second floor apartment. Then I went out to a party.

After a long evening of partying, I got home about 2:00 a.m. and fell asleep. About three hours later, I was awakened by a terrible thrashing and crashing. It sounded as if someone were trying to break in through the sliding glass doors on my balcony. My head still ached from drinking red wine, and getting up after only three hours of sleep was the last thing I wanted to do. I reluctantly crawled from bed and pulled the curtains back to have a look.

It can take several seconds for the human retina to tell the brain what it is seeing. It actually took a bit longer than that in my hung over state. It finally registered that I was looking at a turkey carcass, traveling across my balcony at breakneck speed. Then it would come to a crashing halt as it made greasy contact with the apartment wall or the sliding glass door. For a moment I had the hangover-induced, surreal thought that maybe I really hadn't cooked it fully and it had come back to life.

Then I took another look. What was propelling the turkey were two furry, orange-striped legs. A half-turkey, half-cat combination.

Morris's head and upper body was stuck in the cavity of the turkey. He must have been trying to get some of the offal and gotten lodged inside. And in his frenzy to break free he was ramming the walls with the turkey carcass.

Anyone who has ever tried to rescue a frantic cat knows what a thankless task this can be. The only thing I had going for me was that the front claws were safely ensconced inside the turkey. The trouble was, I couldn't catch him. The cat could hear me but he was in such a panic that anything was a threat. His only chance of survival would be to get away as fast as possible. Which he did.

With a thrust of his powerful, jacked-up hind legs, he leaped to the balcony railing, paused for a second as he teetered with the turkey headdress still in place, and sailed over the edge.

I cringed, then walked over to the balcony and looked down, certain that he'd have blown at least one of his lives. But there he sat, somewhat dazed, shaking his head to free the turkey stuffing from his ears. Then he did what any self-respecting cat would have done. He began to clean himself.

Versatile Meat Sauce

1/4 cup olive oil
1 tbsp chopped garlic (or 4 cloves)
1 cup chopped onion
1 cup chopped celery
1 cup sliced mushrooms
1 cup chopped green pepper
1 lb lean ground beef
1/4 cup chopped parsley
7 cups chopped, skinned fresh tomatoes, with juice (or 2--28 oz cans)
2 (6 oz) cans tomato paste
2 tbsp salt
1/4 tsp paprika
1/4 cayenne
1 tsp basil
1/2 tsp oregano
1 tsp sugar
1 tsp pepper
2 bay leaves

In an extra large pot heat oil, add all the vegetables and simmer until translucent. Add beef and cook until no pink is showing. Add remaining ingredients and simmer for at least an hour. Use over spaghetti or other pasta, or as the meat sauce in lasagna. This sauce can be frozen and thawed for use in any recipe that calls for meat sauce.

Lasagna

Versatile Meat Sauce
Lasagna noodles
Grated Mozzarella cheese
Ricotta cheese
Grated Parmesan cheese
Spinach, cooked and drained (optional)**

The above ingredients have been left without measurements as you may wish to increase/decrease the size of the lasagna. If you have extra ingredients you might want to make another one to freeze for later.

Heat oven to 350 F. Grease an 8 x 8" baking dish (or 9 x 13"), then spoon in a thin layer of Meat Sauce. Cover with a meat sauce with a layer of lasagna noodles, overlapping slightly. Cover noodles with another layer of meat sauce, then a layer of mozzarella cheese. Cover the mozzarella layer with ricotta cheese. Sprinkle parmesan cheese over the ricotta layer, then cover with another layer of noodles. Repeat with another layer of meat sauce, mozzarella, ricotta and parmesan. Top with another layer of noodles, then a layer of meat sauce.

Sprinkle parmesan in a fancy design on top. Bake for 30 minutes or until golden brown on top. Remove from oven and let sit at least 15 minutes to rest.

**If you add spinach, place a thin layer over each meat sauce layer, with the exception of the last (top) layer of meat sauce.

Pineapple Chicken

2 chicken breasts, cut into 1/2" cubes
1/2 cup flour
2 eggs
1 tsp salt
1/4 tsp pepper

Beat together eggs, flour, salt and pepper. Dip cut up chicken into flour mixture and deep fry in hot oil, slowly until brown.

Sauce

1 chicken bouillon cube, dissolved in 1 cup water
1/2 cup pineapple chunks
1 cup pineapple juice
3/4 cup white sugar
1/3 cup vinegar
3 tbsp cornstarch
1/4 water

Bring first 5 ingredients to a boil and add cornstarch mixture. Stir until thickened. Remove from heat and pour over chicken. Serve with white rice.

Chicken Pie

This is the most delicious, delicate chicken pie ever. If you'd prefer to make a large version rather than individual pies, the quantities given here will make one 8" or 9" pie. I like breast meat, but you can use an equal amount of dark if you prefer, or even leftover chicken or turkey.

1 lb boneless chicken breasts
1 3/4 cups chicken stock or canned broth
2 3/4 cups flour
salt and pepper
6 oz. butter, chilled
1/3 cup vegetable shortening
3 carrots
1/2 lb. mushrooms
1/2 tsp. dried thyme
1 cup light cream
2 scallions
2 tbsp. chopped fresh parsley
1 egg

Put chicken breasts in a frying pan with ½ cup stock. Cover and bring to a simmer. Reduce heat and continue simmering, turning once, until chicken is just cooked through, about five minutes. Remove chicken, let cool and tear into pieces. Strain broth and reserve.

Combine 2 1/2 cups of the flour and 3/4 tsp salt. Cut in 1/4 lb of the butter and the shortening until the mixture resembles coarse meal.

Toss in 7 - 8 tbsp cold water, a tablespoon at a time. When the ingredients begin to clump together, press into a ball, wrap and refrigerate. (Continued on Page 48)

Chicken Pie
(Continued from Page 47)

Cut carrots in half lengthwise and then into approximately 1/4 inch slices. Bring to a boil in a large pot of salted water and cook until tender, about five minutes. Drain. Slice mushrooms. In a large saucepan, melt remaining 4 Tbsp butter over medium heat. Add mushrooms, thyme, 1 tsp salt and ½ tsp pepper. Cook until tender, about five minutes.

Stir in remaining 1/4 cup flour and cook 1 minute. Gradually stir in reserved chicken-cooking liquid, remaining 1 1/4 cups stock and the cream. Bring to a boil and cook 1 minute, stirring all the while. Remove from heat, pour off 1 1/2 cups sauce and reserve. Chop scallions. Stir chicken, carrots, scallions, pimento and parsley into the remaining sauce.

Heat oven to 425 F. Beat the egg with 1 Tbsp water. Divide the dough into 2 pieces (12 if you're doing individual pies). On a lightly-floured surface, roll them and fit into pans. Fill with the chicken mixture. Roll the remaining dough, top pie and flute edges. Cut vents in the top crusts.

Brush tops lightly with egg mixture. Put pie on a baking sheet and bake until golden brown, about 35 minutes. Brush tops of pies again with egg mixture after 15 minutes.

6 servings individual pies (with an 8" pie, I get 8 servings)

I have used leftover turkey in this recipe and it's *almost* as good, just a little dry. (I'd add more of the reserved sauce, reserving only 1 cup.) Often what I do is plan ahead to have leftover chicken and carrots. Then I just add everything else as needed.

Cornish Pasties

1/2 lb lean ground beef
2 large onions, chopped finely
2 cups grated potato
1/4 cup chopped parsley
1 tsp salt
2 tsp lemon pepper

Perfect Pastry

1 egg
1 tbsp water

Brown beef in a large skillet, breaking into small pieces with the back of a spoon. Remove with a slotted spoon. Pour off all but 1/4 cup of the droppings. Sauté onion until soft in pan drippings, stir in potato and cook 3 minutes longer. Remove from heat, stir in meat, chopped parsley, salt and pepper. Cool while rolling pastry.

Cut pastry into large circles, place filling onto center. Moisten edges with water, then pinch to seal. Prick with a fork to allow steam to escape. Place on greased cookie sheet. Brush tops with egg and water mixture and bake at 400 F for 20 minutes until pastry is golden. Cool completely on wire rack.

Shepherd's Pie

3 – 4 cups chopped or coarsely ground, leftover roast beef
2 cups gravy (leftover is fine, or from a mix)
1/4 cup finely chopped onions
1 tsp salt
1 tsp pepper
3 – 4 cups cooked mashed potatoes
1/2 tsp paprika

Mix chopped roast beef, chopped onion, salt, pepper and gravy together. Place in 2 quart greased casserole dish. Place mashed potatoes on top of beef mixture. Sprinkle with paprika. Bake at 350 F for 30 minutes.

Note: 1 cup chopped cooked vegetables such as corn, carrots or peas may be added before the potato layer to make a nutritious, colorful meal.

FIRE OVER BRITAIN

Over the years I've hosted hundreds of dinner parties. Dinner clubs have formed with various groups of friends, and almost like a sitcom, spinoff groups of these friends. Many of the dinners have centered around a certain theme or ritual, such as a holiday. But be forewarned: if you do this once, the next year around the same time you'll have friends saying, 'Are you doing that . . . . again this year?" And before you know it, you're stuck with an annual event.

Such was the case with a former coworker of mine. She and her husband were expatriate Britons. They had served in the Royal Air Force together where they mapped flight plans over India. She and I worked for an employment agency; her husband was a city policeman. They lived out of town on a small acreage that gave them plenty of leeway for throwing large, noisy parties.

Each year, on a weekend in July they would host their annual "Pim's Party" named after Pim's Punch, a nasty gin-based alcoholic beverage enjoyed primarily by English people. The usual request was for guests to bring a bottle of Pim's gin, which would then be added to the punch concoction that had been steeping for days with lemons and oranges. The hosts provided all the food, and in homage to their time spent in India, every dish was curried.

The majority of the guests were coworkers and acquaintances of both husband and wife, therefore they were comprised of mostly policemen and fireman. The former can often be formidable partygoers, and like an episode of Survivor, they 'Outdrink, Outplay, Outlast' everyone else. And the Pim's Party was no exception.

Now the Brits love curry, as do I, but my ex husband did not. In fact, he disliked curry so much that if I cooked it in my kitchen he would stay away for days until the smell went away. However, he did enjoy a party, but to attend a curry dinner party he would have to eat. As he wouldn't stay at home and he wouldn't eat curry, I packed a tuna sandwich in an innocuous bag and away we went.

The party was already in full swing when we got there. By full swing, I mean that the policemen were inebriated enough that they were firing their service revolvers into the air at nothing in particular. The firemen seemed to be a quieter lot, content to just watch and wait for injuries or fatalities before they made a move.

A long buffet table had been set with a variety of Indian curry dishes, each a deeper khaki than the next. The depth of the green, I came to understand, was indication of how strong the curry was in the dish. And there was a huge selection.

"How did you manage to cook all this?" I asked my friend, gazing in amazement at the variety.

"Our Jamaican housekeeper starts several weeks ahead of time, then freezes it, so all we have to do is thaw and reheat," she replied.

Now I happen to know, and maybe this was where I learned it, that when you freeze a spicy dish, it becomes spicier than it had been originally. I don't know why this is, probably because the freezing process reduces the amount of liquid. But this piece of information was kept quiet that night.

In various places around the kitchen and living room were Indian snack foods, most of which I can't remember. Some of them were surprisingly bland, but there was one that looked a little like beef jerky that appealed to me. This, I was told, was Bombay Duck. I snagged a couple of pieces, filled a glass with Pim's Punch and went outside to the deck where the shooting was still going on.

Now Bombay Duck may have originated in Bombay, but it bears no resemblance nor relationship to a duck. It has to be the smelliest, nastiest piece of dried fish ever to draw flies. And dogs. And cats. I don't know what kind of fish it came off of, but I soon learned why it had not been placed outdoors. The animals wouldn't leave me alone. More importantly, I couldn't bring myself to eat any more. What would I do with it? It occurred to me then that I could drop it between the floorboards of the cedar deck. Doing so got rid of the dogs and cats, as well as the duck.

But then I had a new problem.

My hostess came out with a fresh pitcher of Pim's and noticed the dogs digging frantically at the sides of the deck.

"Jack," she said, frowning, "what are those dogs doing? Put them in the dog run." Then she walked back into the house.

Her husband bent over the deck where the three dogs were digging, and fired off a couple of shots to scare them. They didn't pause, just kept digging to get at the Bombay Duck. Apparently annoyed that the dogs weren't paying attention, Jack vaulted over the railing in a single leap, grabbed two of the closest dogs by their collars and hauled them off. They twisted and fought to get back to the deck, but he was stronger and soon had them penned away. No sooner had he gotten back to his guests than the dogs had scurried up the six foot wire walls, leapt the pen and began bawling away again at whatever was under the deck.

This became a source of interest to everyone.

"What do you think is under there?" someone asked.

"Maybe a skunk," someone else volunteered.

"It can't be a wild animal because we're making too much noise; they'd never go under the deck."

I kept my mouth shut. I knew perfectly well what was luring those dogs. And it wasn't the cats. By now the cats had crawled under the deck, feasting grandly on the Bombay Duck, which probably fulfilled a multitude of cat needs. Relieved, I took my first swig of Pim's. Then I began to choke.

It tasted like straight grain alcohol with a little lemon in it to soothe the pain. The burn began at my nostrils and extended right down to my pelvis. I can think of no other alcoholic beverage that has ever done this to me. And it wasn't as if it tasted good, either. It was really quite horrible. The only salvation was the lemon floating in my glass, which I promptly ate.

By now it was time for dinner and we lined up, plates in hand, to sample the various Indian dishes that had been so painstakingly prepared. Gary didn't line up. He was sitting in the kitchen trying to be inconspicuous while devouring the tuna sandwich I'd made for him. I grinned weakly, hoping no one would notice. The hostess did. I had to explain that he was allergic to curry.

But as I said, I love curry, and so I loaded my plate right up with all those monochromatic shades of khaki mingling together. Then I sat down to eat.

When a spice such as curry is as strong as it was in those dishes, it is virtually impossible to tell what the rest of the ingredients are. I became convinced that the reason that Indians (and perhaps other cultures as well) heavily spice their foods is because of the lack of refrigeration or proper storage in their home countries. The heavy spice would disguise all ages of meat or other ingredients that may have gone 'off'. This did not make me feel very well.

As none of the dishes were labeled, I soon lost track of what the hostess told us were in them. Some were beef, some lamb, some chicken, but mostly, mystery meat. If you caught a glimpse of a piece of meat, you might have been able to tell what it was by the size or texture. But that would have been the only way.

I took a tentative mouthful of the lightest khaki. The heat of that curry could have melted asphalt. Without thinking I took a large swallow of the Pim's the way someone would gulp water. The burn was intense. Like putting out fire with gasoline. My eyes watered, my nose burned and for a moment it seemed as if all the arteries in my body were responding to the spice. I tingled to my fingertips.

I glanced around to see how everyone else was doing. They were all eating the curry with gusto: they'd been here before. Slipping my plate behind a lamp, I stood up to look for my ex husband so we could make our excuses and get home before Hell and Damnation took over my body. Then I saw him.

On the other side of the room, my ex husband, now sated with bread and tuna, was forgoing the Pim's and asking the hostess if she had a beer. That was the last year we were invited to the Pim's party. But I still love curry.

Indian Fry Bread

1/4 tsp salt
4 tbsp shortening
2 cups whole wheat flour
1 cup white flour
1 cup water

Oil for frying

Mix first 5 ingredients and knead into a ball. Roll out to 1/4" and cut in 4" circles. Heat oil in a pan and test temperature by putting a small cube of bread in. When it browns quickly the oil is hot enough. Carefully place only enough dough circles in so as not to crowd. They will quickly rise to the top of the oil and start to puff up in the center.

Gently push them back into the oil with a slotted wooden spoon. Turn them over when they become light brown and cook the other side. Remove from oil immediately and drain on paper towels. Repeat until all dough is used. Serve with Mulligatawny or other Indian dishes.

Onions au Gratin

3 cups sliced raw onions (sweet onions like Walla Walla or Vidalia are best)
2 tbsp flour
1/2 tsp salt
Dash of pepper
1 1/2 cups grated cheddar cheese
1 tbsp butter
1 tbsp water
1/4 cup buttered bread crumbs

Arrange one cup sliced onion in greased baking dish. Mix flour, cheese and seasonings. Sprinkle 1/3 of flour mixture over onions, then sprinkle with water. Repeat layers twice. Dot with butter. Bake, covered at 350 F until tender, about 30 minutes. Uncover, sprinkle with buttered crumbs and return to oven until brown, about 10 minutes more.

For variations on this you can substitute broccoli or cauliflower in place of the onions.

Crustless Quiche Lorraine

9 – 10 slices cooked and crumbled bacon (or 1 cup chopped cooked ham)
1 cup shredded Swiss or cheddar cheese
1/4 cup minced onion
4 eggs
1 1/2 cup cream
3/4 tsp salt
1/4 tsp sugar
1/8 tsp cayenne

Sprinkle bacon, cheese and onion in a 9" glass pie plate. Beat eggs, cream and seasonings until well blended. Pour over bacon mixture. Bake at 350 F for 45 minutes or until knife inserted in center comes out clean. Let rest for 5 minutes.

If a bottom crust is desired for a heartier meal, line the pie plate with uncooked pie crust and finish as above.

Chicken and Broccoli Quiche

Substitute 1/2 cup chopped chicken or turkey and 1/2 cup cooked, chopped and drained broccoli for the ham. Finish as above.

Seafood Quiche

Substitute cooked 2 cans crabmeat or other seafood for the ham and finish as above.

Blender Croissants

5 cups flour
1 cup very cold butter
1 pkg active dry yeast
1 cup warm water
3/4 cup cream
1 1/2 tsp salt
1/3 cup sugar
1 egg
1/4 cup butter, melted & cooled
1 egg beaten with 1 tbsp water

Put 4 cups of flour in food processor. Cut butter in 1/2 inch squares and distribute over flour. Process on pulse using short on-off bursts until butter particles are the size of peas. Transfer to a large mixing bowl.

Process yeast and water with 2 on-off bursts. Add cream, salt, sugar, egg, the remaining 1 cup flour and melted butter. Process until batter is smooth. Pour over butter-flour mixture. With spatula, carefully turn over mixture and roll out into a circle. Cut into pie-shaped wedges, then roll up to create croissants. Place on a greased baking sheet. Bake at 350 F until golden brown. Do not over bake.

Szechuan Beef

1 lb round or sirloin steak (an expensive cut is not needed)
1 egg, beaten
6 tbsp cornstarch
1/4 cup water

Cooking oil

Sauce

3 carrots (cut into thin, 1/4" x 2" strips)
4 tbsp grated ginger root
4 cloves garlic, chopped
3 green onions (cut into 1/2" sections)
3 tbsp soy sauce
2 tbsp red cooking wine
2 tbsp white vinegar
1 tbsp sesame oil
1/2 cup sugar
1/2 tsp chili flakes
2 tsp cornstarch

Slice steak into thin strips, approximately 1/2" x 2". Mix cornstarch with water and egg, then add to beef. Place in freezer while heating oil in a wok or frying pan to boiling point. Add beef, cooking only about 1 cup at a time, separating it while it's cooking so it doesn't clump. Leave the remainder in the freezer until ready to cook as you will get a crispier product. Remove, drain and set aside.

To make the sauce put the sesame oil in a wok, add carrots, ginger and garlic. Stir fry over high heat. Add remaining ingredients and bring to a boil. Add beef, mix well and serve with steamed white rice.

Beef Wellington

1 4-lb beef tenderloin fillet
1 tsp pepper
1/4 cup softened butter
1 onion, sliced
1 carrot, sliced
1 stalk celery, sliced
4 oz liver pate
1 cup finely chopped mushrooms
1 tsp rosemary leaves

Perfect Pastry

1 egg yolk
1 tbsp water

Spread surface of meat all over with softened butter. Arrange sliced onion, carrot and celery in bottom of roasting pan. Place meat on top of vegetables. Back 40 to 45 minutes in preheated 450 F oven. Remove from oven, cool completely. Discard vegetables. Combine liver pate, mushrooms and rosemary leaves. Spread top and sides of cooled beef with pate mixture.

Roll pie crust out to 18" x 15" and wrap around beef, pressing seams at the bottom with water to seal. Trim edges of pastry. Brush with egg yolk beaten with water. Bake 20 to 25 minutes in preheated 425 F oven, or until pastry is puffed and golden brown. Serves 8.

Cabbage Rolls

1 lb lean ground beef
2 cups cooked white rice
Salt and pepper to taste
One head cabbage
1 large can tomato sauce

The night before, wash the head of cabbage, remove core and dry thoroughly, then stick in freezer. The next day plunge it into boiling water until leaves are limp and pull away easily from head. Do not overcook. The freezing and blanching make them pliable enough to stuff and roll easily.

Cook rice according to directions on package. Cool. Brown the ground beef on medium heat, breaking it up frequently with a wooden spoon to keep it from forming large lumps. Remove from heat and drain any remaining fat. Add cooked white rice to the ground beef, add salt and pepper to taste. Mix well.

Take one cabbage leaf at a time (if necessary, remove any thick, heavy base of the leaf) and place two tablespoons into center. Roll tightly from base end to the top, tucking leaf inwards along the sides as you roll. Place seam side down in a greased 9 x 12" baking pan. Cover with tomato sauce. Bake at 350 F for 30 minutes or until cabbage is fork tender.

Perogys

6 cups flour
1/4 tsp baking powder
2 tsp sugar
2 tbsp cooking oil
1/2 to 1 cup boiling water
1 tbsp salt
2 eggs
1 1/2 cup milk

Mix all dry ingredients, then add the wet. Add water last, using just enough to work together with hands to make a smooth dough. Roll out fairly thin (1/4"), cut in circles about 4". Fill 1 piece with 1 tbsp filling, then moisten sides, fold dough over and pinch to seal. Do not prick. (Fillings are on Page 72)

Cooking

Perogys may be boiled or deep fried. Pan fry to warm as leftovers.

Boiling: Cook about 10 minutes in salted water or until each rises to the top. Remove and drain. Brown chopped onions in butter and pour over; serve with sour cream.

Deep frying: Fry in deep fat heated to about 365 F until golden brown. Remove and serve.

Perogys
(Continued from Page 71)

Cheese filling

1 lb dry cottage cheese
2 egg yolks
3/4 tsp salt.

Mix well until blended.

Potato and cheese filling

3 tbsp butter
2 onions chopped
2 cups mashed potatoes
1 egg
1 cup grated cheddar cheese
1 1/2 tsp salt
1/4 tsp pepper

Melt butter in pan, sauté onion for 15 minutes. Mix all ingredients together until smooth.

Fruit filling

3 cups pitted cherries with juice
1 cup sugar
1 tbsp lemon juice
1 tbsp cornstarch

In a saucepan, combine cherries, sugar, lemon juice and cornstarch. Cook over low heat for 5 minutes. Remove cherries from juice and cornstarch and reserve for garnish. Use cooked cherries to fill perogy dough.

Tourtiere (French Canadian meat pie)

1 lb lean ground pork
1/2 pound lean ground beef
1 small onion, chopped fine
3/4 tbsp butter
1/3 cup warm water
1 tsp salt
Ground black pepper
1 tbsp mixed herbs: parsley, sage, rosemary & thyme (really!)

Perfect Pastry

1 egg

1 tbsp water

Sauté onion lightly in butter, then add meat to which the seasoning has been added. Add water. Cook slowly until meat is done and no pink remains. Cool. Line a pie plate with pastry, sprinkle lightly with flour, add meat, then top with pastry. Brush top with water and egg mixture.

Bake at 400 F for about 10 minutes, brush with egg mixture again. Reduce heat to 350 F and continue baking another 30 minutes.

Brown Sugar Sauce

My mother used to make this and serve it warm over warm Lazy Daisy Cake. Yum!

1 cup light brown sugar
2 tbsp flour
1 1/2 cups water
1 tbsp butter
1 tsp vanilla

Mix the brown sugar and flour with water. Bring to a boil, stirring constantly until thick. Add butter and vanilla.

WHAT BOOB MADE THIS CAKE?

When we were younger, my mother raised chickens. She also raised ducks and geese, without any plan as to what she would do with the resulting eggs. Before too long she had a surplus of enormous duck and goose eggs, but with no real market for them. The goose eggs actually posed no problems. You had to be able to get them away from the goose to use them. We couldn't. When the geese weren't laying, we kids thought it was funny to put light bulbs in their nest. Frighteningly maternal, those geese would sit on the light bulbs for months, trying to get them to hatch. We never got tired of that joke. Payback for all the times they'd chased us, hissing as geese do with their necks snaked out, pecking at our little legs.

The ducks were different. Ducks (except for the mess they left everywhere) made sweet and friendly pets. But their eggs were large and the thought of eating them in an omelet or other 'eggy' dish didn't appeal much to us. So Mom went into her 'experimental' baking phase.

She soon discovered that the quickest way to use up eggs was to make angel food cakes. The recipe called for a dozen eggs. Obviously, with the size of ducks eggs you could actually use fewer. But Mom was trying to get rid of the surplus eggs. So she would use at least twelve to fourteen each time she baked one, which led to angel food cakes so tall that even when the pan was placed on the bottom rack, they still stuck to the inside top of the oven.

After a while though, Mom began to get bored. No longer satisfied with white cakes, she started adding food coloring. It was not unusual to see one of us girls opening our lunch pails to find a huge slice of mauve cake, or robin-egg blue, or (and here is where I drew the line) emerald green cake. Eventually, we were sick to death of angel food cakes and unfortunately, our need to dispose of them came to an abrupt end. A wild mink ended the lives of our entire flock of ducks and there were no more eggs.

As I've mentioned, I come from a long line of bakers, and in fact, I've always been a better baker than a cook. After I moved away from home, if a friend or relative had occasion to need a cake, I volunteered my services. When my sister-in-law planned a large party to celebrate my brother-in-law's thirtieth birthday, it seemed only the natural thing to do to offer to bake the then popular 'boob cake.' Yet I would go one step further. I would make a 'torso cake.'

Now amateur bakers would decide right off to go out hunting for a mold to pour the batter into. With no porn baking shops in the city (actually, I don't know this for sure as I never looked) I realized that the chances of finding a cake pan in the shape of a woman's body would be next to impossible. A rectangular cake, contoured accordingly, would do the trick. The other two "parts" would be baked in metal funnels that would give them their unique conical shape.

After baking the first rectangular cake and allowing it to cool, I cut it into a curvy, female shape. I then lined my one copper funnel with tin foil and balanced it inside the hollow tube of an angel food cake tin. Unfortunately, I neglected to take into account that the depth of the batter would ultimately affect the baking time. When I tested the cake with a toothpick, it came out clean. Assuming the cake was done, I loosened the foil and inverted the funnel on top of the appropriate section of the torso cake. But when I removed the funnel, hot, molten chocolate cake batter burst from the cone and ran, lava-like, down the sides of the table.

I panicked. In spite of the 350 degree temperature of the batter I scooped the whole mess up with my bare hands, thrust it back into the funnel and placed it in the oven again. This time I baked the living tar out of that cake. When I finally took it out of the oven and inverted it back on the torso it stood firmer than any Dow Corning implants. Success! Ignoring the temptation to go out and buy a prosthesis for the other side, I repeated the process. I felt like Dr. Frankenstein of the kitchen. A body was beginning to take shape.

After experimenting with flesh colored frosting for a couple of hours, eventually I ended up with a diverse, multi-cultural color. I slathered the whole cake with it, put some frilly blue frosting panties on the bottom and created luscious chocolate nipples. It looked good enough to eat. Only I knew that it was hard and tough because of the length of baking time. It probably tasted terrible.

When I took it to the party that evening, everyone was truly impressed. Then the somewhat inebriated 30-year-old birthday boy took one look at the cake and plunged his face between the 'breasts'. As he rubbed his face back and forth in the frosting I realized then that I need not have worried about the edibility.

Carrot Cake

4 eggs, well beaten
1 cup vegetable oil
1 1/3 cup white sugar

Beat above ingredients well, then add:

2 cups grated raw carrots
1/2 cup chopped nuts
1/2 cup coconut
1/2 cup raisins (optional)
1 tsp vanilla

Sift together and fold into above mixture:

2 cups all purpose flour
1 tsp salt
1 1/2 tsp soda
1 1/2 tsp baking powder
2 tsp cinnamon

Bake at 325 F for about 50 minutes in a greased 8 x 13 inch cake pan. Frost with broiled or cream cheese frosting.

Broiled Frosting

3 tbsp butter, melted
3/4 cup brown sugar
1/4 cup chopped nuts
2 tbsp milk

Mix together, then spread on cake immediately and return to oven for 10 minutes.

Cream Cheese frosting

1 package cream cheese (8 oz) softened
1 tsp vanilla
2 cups icing sugar (powdered)

With electric mixer, beat cream cheese until flurry. Beat in vanilla, then add icing sugar, 1/2 cup at a time, until smooth and creamy. Spread on cooled cake.

Harvest Ribbon Cake

2 1/2 cups sifted cake flour
1 tsp salt
1 2/3 cups granulated sugar
2/3 cup butter
3/4 cup milk
4 1/2 tsp baking powder
1 tsp vanilla
1/2 cup milk
5 egg whites

Heat oven to 360 F. Grease, then line with waxed paper, bottoms of three 1 ¼" deep, 8" layer pans. Into large mixer bowl, sift flour, salt and sugar. Drop in butter. Pour in 3/4 cup milk. With mixer at low to medium speed, beat 2 minutes, scraping bowl and beaters when necessary. Stir in baking powder. Add vanilla, 1/2 cup milk, egg whites. Beat 2 minutes longer.

Divide batter into 3 parts.

For yellow layer

Yellow food color
1 tbsp orange rind

Add a few drops yellow food coloring and 1 tbsp grated orange rind. Fold into one third of the batter.

For chocolate layer

1/2 tsp cinnamon
1/8 tsp powdered cloves
1/8 tsp baking soda
2 tbsp cocoa blended with 2 tbsp water (Continued on Page 73)

Harvest Ribbon Cake (Continued from Page 72)

Mix all ingredients and fold into one third of the batter.

Turn the batter into the three prepared pans. Bake about 20 – 25 minutes, or until done. Cool in pans on wire racks 10 minutes. Remove from pans, peel off paper, cool on racks. Fill and frost layers with Sea Foam Frosting.

Decorate outer top edge with 5 sprays of dark raisins, alternated with 5 piles of toasted almonds (6 in a pile), letting both extend down cake sides a bit. Just before serving, sprinkle with a bit of grated orange rind (or toasted coconut) over the almonds.

Sea Foam Frosting

1 cup plus 2 tbsp Roger's Golden Syrup (or dark corn syrup)
3 egg whites
1 1/2 tsp vanilla
Pinch of salt

In a small saucepan, heat syrup till boiling. With electric mixer at high speed, beat egg whites in a mixing bowl until stiff but not dry, add salt. Slowly pour syrup over egg whites, beating until frosting is fluffy and hangs in peaks from beater, add vanilla. Fills and frosts three 8" layers.

Lazy Daisy Cake

2 eggs, beaten
1 cup sugar
2 tbsp butter
1/2 cup scalded milk
1 cup flour
1 tsp baking powder
1/4 tsp salt
1 tsp vanilla

Sift together flour, baking powder and salt. Beat eggs until very light, add sugar gradually, beating until thick and lemon-colored. Fold dry ingredients into egg mixture, gently but thoroughly. Combine butter and scalded milk. Stir in vanilla. Add to first mixture, stirring until well blended. Turn into greased 8" square pan. Bake in moderate oven, 350 F. for 30 minutes, or until done.

This makes a wonderful snack cake, or a base cake for desserts such as strawberry shortcake.

Marshmallow Dreams

1 cup graham wafer crumbs
2 cups dates, cut fine
2 cups mini marshmallows
1 cup whipped cream
1 cup chopped nuts
1 cup maraschino cherries
Pinch of salt
1 tsp vanilla
1/2 tsp almond extract

Place all ingredients in bowl and mix with hands. Fold in whipped cream last. Form into small balls, roll in coconut or chocolate shot. Store in refrigerator.

Nutcracker Suite Cake (Germany)

6 eggs, separated
1 cup sugar
1/4 cup sifted flour
1 1/4 tsp baking powder
1 tsp cinnamon
1/2 tsp cloves
2 tbsp vegetable oil
2 tsp rum extract
1 cup graham cracker crumbs
1 square unsweetened grated chocolate
1 cup chopped nuts
2 cups whipping cream
1/2 sifted powdered sugar

Heat oven to 350 F. Line bottom of two layer cake pans or an oblong pan with aluminum foil. In large mixing bowl beat egg whites until frothy. Gradually add 1/2 cup sugar, flour, baking powder, cinnamon, cloves, egg yolks, oil and 1 tsp rum extract. Beat for 1 minute. Pour egg yolk mixture over egg whites. Gently fold with spatula until blended. Fold in crumbs, chocolate and nuts.

Pour into pans. Bake for 30 – 40 minutes. Invert to cool completely. Whip cream with 1/2 cup powdered sugar until stiff, add 1 tsp rum extract. Spread one half of whipped cream over one layer, then stack the second layer on top. Garnish top with remaining whipped cream and grated chocolate.

Blueberry Muffins

1/2 cup sugar
1/2 cup butter, softened
1 egg, well beaten
1 tsp vanilla
1 3/4 cups flour
4 tsp baking powder
1/2 tsp salt
1 cup milk
2 cups fresh blueberries (or frozen, unthawed)
1/2 cup flour (to add to blueberries)

In a mixing bowl, cream sugar and butter until fluffy. Beat in the egg and vanilla. In a separate bowl combine the 1 3/4 cups flour, baking powder and salt. Add the dry ingredients to the sugar and egg mixture alternately with the milk. Beat well. Mix 1/2 cup flour with blueberries and fold into the batter. Sprinkle topping over batter and bake at 375 F for 20 to 25 minutes or until golden.

Topping

1/2 cup sugar
1/2 tsp cinnamon
2/3 cup flour
1/2 cup butter

Mix the sugar, cinnamon, flour and butter until crumbly. Finish as above.

Tropical Banana Bread

1 cup flaked coconut
1/3 cup butter
2/3 cup sugar
2 eggs
3 tbsp milk
1/2 tsp almond extract
1/4 tsp vanilla
2 cups flour
1 tsp baking powder
1/2 tsp baking soda
1/2 tsp salt
1 cup mashed bananas (three small)

Heat oven to 350 F. Spread coconut on cookie sheet and bake until golden brown, then remove from heat. Combine butter, sugar and eggs, beat until fluffy. Stir in milk, almond and vanilla extract. Sift flour, baking powder, soda and salt together. Add to first mixture alternately with the mashed bananas. Fold in toasted coconut. Spoon mixture into a greased loaf pan.

Bake about 50 minutes or until center is no longer wet when tested with a toothpick. Turn out of pan and place on a rack to cool.

Carrot Pineapple Muffins

1 1/2 cups flour
1 cup white sugar
2/3 cup oil
2 eggs
1 cup grated carrots
1/2 cup crushed pineapple (drained)
1 tsp cinnamon
1 tsp baking powder
1 tsp baking soda
1 tsp salt
1 tsp vanilla

Beat eggs with oil, add vanilla. Mix dry ingredients, then fold into egg mixture. Drop mixture into lined muffin pans. Bake at 350 F for 15-20 minutes.

Oatmeal Raisin Cookies

3/4 cup butter
1 1/4 cups brown sugar
1 egg
1 1/2 cups oatmeal
1 cup coconut
1 cup flour
1/2 tsp baking soda
1/2 tsp baking powder
1/2 tsp salt
1 tsp vanilla
1 cup raisins

Mix first three ingredients together with electric mixer. Sift dry ingredients together. Add to butter/sugar mixture and beat until well mixed. Stir in vanilla and raisins. Roll into 1" balls. Do not flatten. Bake at 350 F for 8 - 10 minutes, or until golden brown on bottom. Do not over bake.

OF MEN AND MACHINES

There are a lot of men who enjoy cooking and puttering around the kitchen. My ex husband was not one of these. However, he was innately fascinated by household appliances because they had a motor. All my new appliances had to be personally inspected and approved by him for performance, speed and durability beforehand. If I bought one without his approval, he'd take it apart before I used it to see how it worked. Often I ended up with much more of a product than I needed, such as the industrial strength mixer I received from him for Christmas, which could mix up enough bread dough at one time to fill a bakery shelf.

Of course, the appliances I owned before we met fell far short of his expectations. Fascinated by the cookie presses that extrude perfect cookies in various shapes, I had once bought a manual cookie press. But it was hard work squeezing stiff cookie dough. So I was delighted to find an electric cookie gun, with lots and lots of templates, tubes and recipes.

One day I decided to whip up a batch of cookies and use my cookie gun for shaping. As soon as Gary heard the 'whiiiirrrr-plop,' whiiiirrr-plop,' of my cookie press, painfully grunting out perfect little rosettes, he came running.

"I can make that work faster," he said eagerly. My heart sank.

"It's fine just the way it is," I said, not looking up as I kept up the rhythm of 'whiiiirrrr-plop', 'whiiiirrrr-plop'. If you stopped in the middle, the cookies kept coming, ready or not, like the chocolate assembly-line episode from "I Love Lucy."

"That motor's going to burn out soon if I don't work on it," he warned. I sighed heavily, knowing I might as well give in.

"Just let me finish with the rest of the dough and then you can have it," I said, "and if you break it, you're going to buy me another one."

You could just see his eyes light up. So while my cookies baked, he opened up the cookie press motor and tinkered and played with it to his hearts content. Then he put it back together.

"Try it now," he said, all excited.

"I don't have any dough left," I said. But he was looking at the unbaked cookies on the cookie sheet. "Stuff that dough back in," he said. "I want to try it out."

I did as he said, it was easier that way, and stuffed the already pressed cookie dough back into the press. He was fairly twitching beside me.

"Let me do it," he said, reaching for the press.

"There's a lot of timing involved with it," I said, getting annoyed now. "It's not as easy as it looks."

But you couldn't deter Gary when he had a plan. He took the cookie gun and began squeezing the trigger. With his tinkering, the former, slow and painful 'whiiiirrrr-plop' had been upgraded to 'whiiiipppp-splat!' as cookies began shooting out left and right.

Surprised, he stopped squeezing, but of course, the momentum behind the dough was still there, and the cookies came out faster than he could line them up on the pan. I grabbed the cookie gun and paced them carefully as the rest of the dough extruded into actual cookie shapes. When the last of the dough emerged I could finally relax my aching arms. I set the gun down on the counter and looked up to see Gary grinning ecstatically.

"See how much better it works now?" he said.

Gingersnaps

1/2 cup butter
1 cup sugar
1 egg
1/4 cup molasses
2 cups flour
2 tsp ginger
1 tsp cinnamon
2 tsp baking soda

Beat first four ingredients together. Add remaining ingredients. Roll into 1" balls, then roll in sugar. Do not flatten. Bake approximately 10 minutes at 350 F.

Fancy Whipped Shortbread

1 lb soft butter
1 cup powdered sugar
3 cups flour
1/2 cup cornstarch
2 tbsp of a favorite liqueur such as Amaretto or Grand Marnier

Sift flour and cornstarch together. Whip butter and powdered sugar, add liqueur. Add flour and corn starch. Drop by spoonfuls onto ungreased baking pan, or extrude with a cookie press. Bake at 350 F until golden on the bottom. Do not over bake.

Chocolate Kiss Cookies

3/4 cup butter, softened
1/2 cup sugar
1 tsp vanilla
1 3/4 cups flour
1 cup finely chopped pecans
1 9 oz package chocolate candies (Hershey's Kisses)
Powdered sugar

Cream butter and sugar with vanilla. Add flour gradually until blended. Stir in nuts. Chill dough. Mold one tbsp around each kiss. Bake at 375 F until golden brown, about 8-10 minutes. Cool before removing from pan. Dust with powdered sugar. These freeze well. Makes approximately 3 dozen.

Chewy Pecan Cookies

1 1/2 cups firmly packed dark brown sugar
1 cup mayonnaise
2 eggs
1 tsp vanilla
2 3/4 cups flour
1/2 tsp baking soda
1/4 tsp salt
1 cup chopped pecans
1 cup pecan halves (optional)

In a large bowl beat first 4 ingredients until smooth. Stir in next 4 ingredients. Drop by tablespoonfuls, 2 inches apart on greased cookie sheets. Top each with a pecan half, if desired. Bake in 375 F oven, 8 to 10 minutes or until lightly browned. Transfer cookies to wire rack. Makes about 4 dozen.

Chewy Chocolate Cookies

3/4 cup butter, softened
2 cups sugar
2 eggs
2 tsp vanilla
2 cups flour
3/4 cup cocoa
1 tsp baking soda
1/2 tsp salt
1 cup finely chopped nuts, optional

Cream butter and sugar in large bowl. Add eggs and vanilla, blend well. Combine flour, cocoa, baking soda and salt. Blend into creamed mixture. Stir in nuts, if desired. Drop by teaspoonfuls onto ungreased cookie sheet. Bake at 350 F. for 8 to 9 minutes. Do not over bake. Cookies will be soft. Cool on cookie sheet until set, about 1 minute. Remove to wire rack to cool completely. Makes about 4 dozen.

Macaroons

4 egg whites
1 1/4 cup sugar
3/4 cup flour
1/2 tsp salt
1/2 tsp vanilla
2 1/2 cup coconut

Heat oven to 350 F. Lightly grease baking sheet. Beat eggs to form stiff but moist peaks. Gradually beat in sugar until stiff and shiny. Stir in flour, salt and vanilla. Fold in coconut. Drop from teaspoon, 2 inches apart. Bake for 10 – 12 minutes or until golden brown. Makes about 4 dozen.

Unbaked Chocolate Cookies

1/2 cup butter
1/2 cup milk
1/2 cup cocoa
2 cups sugar
1 tsp vanilla
3 cups oatmeal
1/2 cup coconut

Mix and boil together first 5 ingredients for 5 minutes, no more. Add 3 cups oatmeal and 1/2 cup coconut. Immediately drop by teaspoonfuls onto greased wax paper. Cool.

Maple Pecan Squares

Base

1 cup flour
1/4 cup brown sugar
1/2 cup butter

Topping

2/3 cup brown sugar
1 cup maple syrup
2 eggs, beaten
1/4 cup butter, softened
1/4 tsp salt
2/3 cup pecan halves
1/2 tsp vanilla
2 tbsp flour

Preheat oven to 350 F. Rub flour, sugar and butter together. Press mixture firmly into 8" square pan. Bake at 350 F for 5 minutes.

Combine sugar and syrup. Simmer 5 minutes, cool slightly. Pour over beaten eggs, stirring well. Stir in remaining ingredients. Spread over partially baked dough. Bake at 450 F for 10 minutes. Reduce heat to 350 F and bake for 20 minutes. Cut into squares when cool.

Oh Henry Bars

Whole graham wafers
1 cup brown sugar
1/2 cup butter
1/2 cup milk
1 1/3 cups graham wafer crumbs
1 cup chopped walnuts
1 cup shredded coconut
1/4 cup maraschino cherries, cut and drained

Icing

1 1/2 cups powdered sugar
3 tbsp butter
1 tbsp plus 2 tsp milk
1/2 tsp vanilla
Red food coloring

Line 9 x 9" pan with whole graham wafers. Trim to fit. Set aside. In sauce pan, combine sugar, butter and milk. Bring to a boil. Let simmer for 2 minutes. Remove. Add wafer crumbs, nuts, coconut and cherries. Mix well. Pour over wafers in pan. Cool.

Beat all Icing ingredients together in a small bowl. If too thin add more sugar; if too thick add more milk. Frost and let stand overnight.

Nanaimo Bars

1/2 cup butter
5 tbsp powdered chocolate
1 cup coconut
1/2 cut chopped walnuts
1/2 tsp vanilla
5 tbsp sugar
2 cups crushed graham wafers
1 egg

Melt butter in top of a double boiler. Add chocolate. Remove from heat. Add the beaten egg and the sugar. Mix well. Add vanilla and other ingredients. Grease a 9" square pan and press this mixture into the bottom of the pan.

Icing

4 tbsp butter
1 tsp vanilla
2 cups sifted powdered sugar
2 tbsp milk

Cream butter, add vanilla. Add sugar and milk alternately, making sure no lumps form. Spread this mixture on top of bottom filling in pan.

Topping

2 squares melted semi-sweet chocolate
1 tbsp butter

Melt together in top of double boiler and spread on icing when thoroughly cooled. Place in refrigerator until ready to serve. Cut in squares.

After Dinner Mint Nanaimo Bars

1 tsp peppermint extract
Green food coloring

Substitute 1 tsp peppermint extract for the vanilla in the icing. Add several drops of green food coloring. Finish as above.

Cherries Jubilee Nanaimo Bars

1/4 cup chopped maraschino cherries
1/2 tsp almond extract
Red food coloring

Substitute almond extract for the vanilla in the icing. Add several drops of red food coloring, Fold in maraschino cherries. Finish as above.

Licorice Caramels

1 cup butter
2 cups granulated sugar
1 14 oz can sweetened condensed milk
1 cup Roger's Golden Syrup (or light corn syrup)
1/8 tsp salt
1 tsp anise extract
1/2 tsp black or red coloring paste (optional)

Line a 9" square baking pan with foil, extending foil over the edges of the pan. Butter the foil; set aside.

In a heavy 3 quart saucepan, melt the butter over low heat. Add the sugar, condensed milk, Roger's syrup and salt. Mix well. Carefully clip a candy thermometer to the side of the pan.

Cook over medium heat, stirring frequently until candy thermometer registers 244 F (firm ball stage). The mixture should boil to a moderate, steady rate over the entire surface. Reaching firm ball stage should take 15 to 20 minutes. (Mixture scorches easily).

Remove from heat, remove thermometer from saucepan. Add anise extract and coloring, stir to mix.

Quickly pour candy, without scraping, into prepared pan. Cool several hours or until firm. Use foil to lift candy out of pan onto cutting board. Peel foil away and discard. With a buttered sharp knife, cut immediately into 1" squares. Wrap in wax paper.

Note: If you do not like licorice, then any other flavor such as vanilla, peppermint, etc., could be substituted in place of the anise extract.

INTO THE MOUTHS OF BABES

There are no high school or college cooking classes that can prepare a new wife for cooking for a husband and children. The only solution I can see would be for a young woman to pay attention to the family dynamics while dinner is being cooked and then listen and learn when everyone else is seated at the dinner table. My sister and I rarely complained about my mother's cooking, but my little brother refused to eat anything but peanut butter and jelly sandwiches for months, even while the rest of the family enjoyed roast beef, mash potatoes, gravy, Yorkshire pudding and dessert. I also remembered saying, "When I have kids, I'm not going to make a separate meal for them." Yeah right.

In retrospect, I think there is a fine, invisible timeline between when your child says 'Yuck, I'm not eating that,' and when they turn to their wives and say, "This isn't how Mom used to make it." Both statements are infuriating, humiliating and likely to get a pan over their head from a less patient parent or spouse.

When my first child was born I began him on solids at the prescribed age of around three months. Actually, he began eating solids on his own about a month earlier as an unfortunate spider happened to cross his path. Any new parent will soon discover that their child has certain favorite foods and they will eat NOTHING else for weeks at a time. This prompts the mother to stock up on that food. That's the time that your child will suddenly take an instant and violent dislike to that food and you will be stuck forever with tiny jars of pureed liver and bacon.

While my son was still a toddler I became more relaxed about what would become of him if I were ever in an accident and unable to feed him. A competent forager, he would peruse the pantry for a half hour at a time, looking for nourishment. He mastered the electric can opener around that time as well. It amazes me now to think back on those times when years later, at the ripe old age of 21, he'd be sitting in front of the television and the first words out of his mouth when I walked through the door after a long day at work was, "What's to eat?"

I relied upon commercial baby foods for only a short time, and then used them only when traveling. With a blender and a microwave, preparing baby foods suddenly became much more efficient. Unless it was excessively spicy or had ingredients I knew would cause Vesuvius to burst through the diaper, I pureed the same food that his father and I ate. As his baby teeth came in, I just chopped meats finely and after a couple of years, of course, he was on grown up food.

As he grew so did his vocabulary and he became a resident food critic. One day I gave him some homemade stew for lunch and washed dishes while he chewed. After the dishes were clean, I swept the floor, folded the laundry, and wiped his high chair tray. He was still chewing. There was practically no food left on his plate, so I wondered at this, but didn't question it. I left the kitchen for a few minutes. When I returned he was still chewing. Finally he reached into his mouth and pulled out a whitish mass.

"Wook, Mommy," he said happily, "meat gum." He'd apparently hit a tough piece.

He also had the ability to put any strawberry, no matter how large, into his mouth whole. This became a challenge to me to see if he wouldn't just once, bite into a strawberry that he thought too large to fit in. I know a conscientious mother wouldn't have done this for fear of her child choking. But strawberries are mostly water anyhow, and I figured if he did begin to choke, I could squish what he couldn't chew.

One day I came home from the store with a basket of strawberries, so large there were only four in the basket. And at the bottom was truly the largest strawberry I have ever seen. It was roughly the size of a small apple. I rinsed it carefully, then held it up to him, tantalizing him with its redness and size. His eyes glowed as he reached for it.

My ex husband and I watched as he pushed it toward his mouth. It was roughly double the size of the opening, but he refused to take a bite. I grabbed my camera and took pictures as we watched him push and push, working the dripping strawberry into his mouth. It took him about two or three minutes, but finally he was done. He'd managed to fit the entire thing in without biting into it. Then he proceeded to chew slowly until it disappeared from sight.

Baking elaborate birthday cakes for my children was one of the most rewarding tasks I undertook during their younger years. I didn't take the coward's way out the way the other parents did and purchase the cake. I made flower garden cakes, Cookie Monster cakes, RV shaped cakes, rainbow cakes with cotton candy clouds. For my daughter's fifth birthday I made an entire castle made of cake.

Now this cake looked fantastic in the book. The turrets were baked in soup cans, and according to the recipe, the Jello called for in the mix gave it a nice texture and a candy-like flavor. They were wrong. It tasted nothing like candy and it was awful cake. But it was pretty rubbery and so you would think it would stay together while I turned cake into a castle.

I'll go on record as saying that cake is not a good medium for building material. For anyone other than a professional baker there is nothing in the constitution of cake that gives it enough strength to be stacked, higher and higher, with no danger of collapse. Such was the case with the castle. I don't know how they got the one in the picture to stay together long enough for the photographer to create the layout, but my first turret fell off before I could even get the second one up. This became very frustrating as I had three more turrets to go. Not to mention decorating the cake.

Using an entire box of toothpicks, I finally had all the turrets, banners, windows, porticos and whatever else embellished the castle, fastened down to FEMA specifications. I further cemented it with the recipe for spackle-type frosting. It would hold together, but only with the benefit of non-edible materials. I would have to make certain that none of the kids would bite into a toothpick.

After the party games, I brought out the castle to the 'oohs' and 'aahhs' of the kids. Then it was time for the candles on the turrets to be lit and to sing, "Happy Birthday." All the children gathered round the table and received a piece of cake. I watched closely to see if it had turned out as poorly as I imagined. Most of the children took one bite. Then, with the limited attention span of five-year-olds began, they began playing with the contents of their 'goodie bags.' But one brave young boy took several mouthfuls, which made me feel much better, and prompted me to ask him how he liked it.

"It looks better than it tastes," he said brightly.

I had to agree with him.

Finger Jello

2 pkg unflavored gelatin
1 six oz package Jello, any flavor
2 1/2 cups water
1/4 cups sugar

Dissolve gelatin in 1 cup of cold water. Set aside. Bring 1 cup of water to a boil and add Jello and sugar. Bring to a boil again and remove from heat. Add the gelatin mixture. Stir and add 1/2 cup of cold water. Pour into a greased 8 x 8" pan. Set in fridge until solid, about 2 hours. Cut into shapes or strips.

Playdough

1 cup flour
1/2 tsp salt
2 tbsp cream of tartar
1 tbsp salad oil
1 cup cool water
Food coloring

Add whatever color of food coloring you wish the playdough to be to the water, then cook all ingredients together on medium heat. Cool, then knead.

Playdough should not stick to the fingers when cool. Store in air tight container. While this dough is for playing, not for eating, it is reassuring to make your own playdough should any inadvertently end up in a child's mouth.

Dill Dip

1 cup mayonnaise
1 cup sour cream
1 tbsp parsley flakes
1 tbsp dill weed
1 tbsp minced onion
1/4 tsp lemon pepper
1 tbsp Bon Appetite (if desired)

Mix well and use for vegetable or chip dip.

Guacamole

2 medium sized ripe avocadoes
1/3 cup mayonnaise
1 tbsp lemon juice
1 tsp salt
1 tsp grated onion
1/4 tsp liquid red pepper seasoning
1 large tomato, peeled, chopped and drained

Halve avocadoes, peel, pit and mash in a medium sized bowl. Blend in remaining ingredients, cover and chill. Dip will stay bright green for several hours.

RODENT FLAMBÉ

Shortly after my family and I moved from Canada to our new home in Lake Oswego, Oregon, one of our neighbors invited us over to spend an evening with them. When my ex husband, Gary, got home from work he asked, "Is the invitation for dinner?"

Now I am an unassuming person and don't like to ask questions like that.

I frowned.

"I don't remember her saying anything about dinner."

"Why don't you call her and ask?" he suggested.

"Oh, I couldn't do that," I replied. "I don't know her very well. And what if it isn't--it'll look like we're inviting ourselves. She'd have no choice but to say it was."

"Well, what if it is?" he asked, sounding exasperated.

I shrugged. "I really doubt that it's a dinner invitation. She said to come over at 7:00 p.m. That's pretty late for dinner. With drinks and hors d'oeuvres you wouldn't start eating 'till at least 8:30 p.m."

He sighed. "Okay, have it your way, but I still think you should call."

So that Saturday night I prepared our dinner, a fairly large one actually, and topped it off with banana splits for dessert. We ate at 5:30 and headed over to Debbie and Dan's house at 7:00 p.m.

Dan answered the door, took our coats and asked what we'd like to drink. He showed us to the living room and we sat while he prepared them. Soon he returned with the drinks, followed closely by Debbie, wearing an apron and carrying two huge plates of hearty hors d'oeuvres.

"I hope you like salmon," she said, wiping her hands on her apron. I glanced at the hors d'oeuvres. There was no salmon anywhere to be seen. Suddenly I had the sinking sensation she was talking about dinner.

Gary glared at me. I ignored him and turned to Debbie.

"We love it," I said. Gary poked me.

"Tell them," he said. I ignored him again.

"No," I grunted, like a ventriloquist, not moving my lips.

"Tell them," he said again.

By this time Debbie and Dan were getting noticeably uncomfortable.

"Tell us what?" said Debbie.

"We already ate," said my ex husband, jerking his thumb at me. "*She* was afraid to ask if you were serving dinner tonight, so she just *assumed* you weren't."

"Didn't I mention dinner?" said Debbie.

I shook my head. "I don't think so."

"Oh," she said, sounding deflated. My ex husband stood up.

"I'm diabetic," he announced. "But it's no problem, I just have to take more insulin." With that he left the house and went back to ours to get another shot.

I was left sitting there with a pained, forced grin on my face.

"It's all right," I said. "We've *always* got room for salmon." And so the evening started off rather awkwardly.

Before too long Gary returned and we all regrouped in the living room. I made a big show of having a lot of the hors d'oeuvres to show my insatiable appetite, made incredibly difficult because I was still so full. Dan watched me, smiling.

"How are you doing the salmon?" I asked, for lack of anything better to say.

"We're barbequing it," he said. "I enjoy barbequing and the salmon turns out really moist that way."

There was another long pause. The conversation was stilted, as if everyone was trying really hard to think up something to say that would take the pressure off our achingly full stomachs.

Suddenly Dan said, "You know, the last time we barbequed we had a really interesting experience."

"Oh?" I said.

Just then Debbie came in from the kitchen.

"Yes," she said, "Dan had just lit the barbeque and we were getting ready to put the salmon on the grill. We heard a funny noise and looked out the kitchen window to see the barbeque shaking back and forth. So Dan went out to the patio and opened the lid. Suddenly a singed possum came flying out." She paused dramatically. "Flames shot off its back as it ran into the bushes."

There was a heavy silence. "We have no idea how it got there," Debbie continued, "but we never saw it again."

"I've never seen a possum move that fast," Dan reflected.

I stared, open mouthed. This was no doubt the same barbeque that our salmon was being cooked upon as we spoke.

"What did your company say?" I asked, swallowing hard.

"Oh, they thought it was pretty funny," Dan said. "You know, complete with Beverly Hillbilly jokes and all. They haven't let us forget it."

I thought for a moment about my full stomach and the flambéed possum dancing on the hot coals where our current dinner now lay. It was definitely getting harder to work up an appetite.

English Trifle

White cake, such as Lazy Daisy, sponge cake, pound cake, or angel food
Jam (raspberry or strawberry)
3 cups miniature marshmallows
3/4 cup milk
2 eggs, beaten
1 cup heavy cream
1 tsp vanilla (or 2 tbsp brandy)
One 14 oz can sliced peaches

Maraschino cherries, if desired (for garnish)

Slowly melt marshmallows with milk, stir, then gradually add beaten eggs. Cook 2 to 3 minutes. Remove from heat, add vanilla or brandy. Chill until thickened. Fold in whipped cream.

Slice cake into 1" slices, spread with jam, then line a large clear glass bowl with the cake. Arrange peach slices over cake, put a layer of the cream mixture over the peaches, then repeat with cake and peaches. Garnish with peaches and maraschino cherries, if desired. Chill overnight.

Pavlova (Australia)

Pavlova is really nothing more than a meringue, filled with fruit and whipped cream. And yet, as one of my Aussie mates once said, "That's a right dinkum Pavlova you got there!"

Meringue

4 egg whites
1 cup white sugar
1/2 tsp vanilla
1 tsp vinegar

2 cups whipping cream
Fresh fruit such as strawberries and/or kiwis
1/2 cup toasted slivered almonds

Whip egg whites until they form stiff peaks, gradually adding sugar a couple of tablespoons at a time. Continue beating and add vanilla and vinegar. Beat until very stiff.

Spread a sheet of brown paper on a cookie sheet and draw a large circle, slightly smaller than the desired size. Bake on hour at 275 F. Turn oven off and allow meringue to dry for several hours.

Top with whipped cream, fruit and toasted almonds.

A fun variation if you're having dinner guests is to make small, individual meringues by drawing smaller circles on the brown paper. Proceed with the whipped cream and fruit to serve.

WHAT A TREAT

One of the things that impending motherhood does not prepare us for are the never-ending time commitments to our family. There are school events, sports events, and family events to plan and attend, not to mention just trying to keep the house from being condemned by the Department of Health. The stress level of homemakers is unrealistically high and women are now just as likely to suffer from strokes or heart attacks as men.

I had been no different than other women in trying to juggle dozens of activities and still maintain my sanity. Not to mention, I had just begun to create a life for myself outside my family and had become involved with horses and a riding club.

One month, I was on my fourth evening meeting for the week and was really too tired to go out one more night. However, as the secretary of the riding group I belonged to, I had to show up and take minutes. Also, I said I'd bring snacks, and since someone else had called me and defaulted, I felt even more obligated. The meeting was to begin at 7 p.m., but I was to set up refreshments a half-hour before that.

There was just one problem. My son had a high school track meet from 4:00 p.m. to 6:30 p.m. Pressed for time, I left the track meet an hour early and ran to the store. There I bought fresh vegetables and Rice Krispies and drove home. I melted some marshmallows and butter and created Rice Krispie Treats, peeled and washed the veggies and made a dip, then prepared a dinner for my family.

By this time it was 6:15 p.m. I had fifteen minutes to get to the meeting and set up. Watching carefully for police cars and being careful not to speed too much, I dashed to the meeting place, ran around to the passenger side of the car, and reached in for the glass pan of Rice Krispie Treats, the tray of vegetables, the dip, my purse, notepad and pen. Carefully, I balanced all these together, then attempted to lock the car door.

Suddenly the Pyrex pan of 'Treats' shot out from underneath my notepad and hit the pavement from a height of about four feet. There was a tremendous crack, but because of the gluey marshmallow concoction inside, nothing separated. But when I lifted the pan, it began to pull apart.

As I picked up glass, and treats, some shards from the pan sliced through my fingers and I started to bleed. Dabbing at the blood, I glanced around to see if anyone had noticed what had just happened. Perhaps there was a way I could restore the food, because there was certainly no time to get anything else.

I tried to pick glass fragments out of RKT's so people wouldn't bleed from their gums if, potentially, I could still pass them off. I'd heard of people eating entire beer glasses without suffering ill effects. But it wouldn't work. Even with my excellent eyesight it was impossible to find the glass fragments stuck between the marshmallow and Rice Krispies.

Then the stress of trying to be everything to everybody finally got to me. I finally went inside and begged someone else to take minutes so I could go home and bawl. Fortunately, someone took pity on me and I headed for home.

Once home, I placed the Rice Krispie Treats on the kitchen counter, turned them upside down and looked at them carefully. I still couldn't see any glass. Now, all good cooks hate waste. And as I love Rice Krispie Treats, I thought, to heck with it, I'm going to resurrect them. I carefully cut off the edges where you could see a few teeny bits of glass shards and I cut them into squares. Then I had a couple. Despite their delicious taste, after two or three of them, you can feel the skin on the roof of your mouth begin to shred.

It suddenly occurred to me that if *I* couldn't tell there was glass in them, I should have served them to the other women. I'll bet they'd never have noticed.

Caramel Popcorn

2 cups brown sugar
1/2 cup Roger's Golden Syrup (or dark corn syrup)
1 cup butter
1 tsp vanilla
1/2 tsp baking soda
Pinch salt

Freshly popped popcorn (approximately 2/3 full of a large roasting pan)

Mix first four ingredients together in a saucepan. Bring to a boil. Boil for 5 minutes. Remove from heat and add vanilla, soda and salt. Pour over popcorn in roasting pan and mix well. Cover and bake at 200 F for one hour, stirring every 15 minutes to prevent clumping.

JUST A HUNKA HUNKA BURNING TOAST

A popular breakfast treat at our house was cinnamon toast. I grew up having cinnamon toast for breakfast when, as a teenager with an enormous appetite, I could down six slices as long as the hot chocolate held out. My son enjoyed it for breakfast, much the same as I did, although not in the same quantities.

Using an old spice bottle, I add cinnamon to sugar until it is a rich brown. I never measure the amount, just check for the depth of color. This is then sprinkled on hot, buttered toast, until the sugar is absorbed by the butter. My rule is: The more butter you use, the more cinnamon sugar you're able to absorb. Your hips then absorb the rest.

One morning, my son Jim requested cinnamon toast for breakfast. I had just laid down on the family room sofa because I'd only had a couple of hours sleep the night before. Gary and I had been arguing about whether or not to buy a house in the country. I was against it because it would mean our teenaged son and daughter would have to spend an extra hour traveling to school on the freeway at rush hour. I am of the opinion that the less time you drive, the less likely you are to be killed in a car crash. It's like a death lottery: the more you play, the more likely you are to win. Or lose. At least that's how I see it.

In any event, I dragged myself off the sofa and went to the spice rack where I kept the cinnamon sugar. I noticed it only had about an inch or so left in the bottle, so I added a teaspoon of cinnamon and filled it up with sugar, shaking it to mix. After toasting the bread, I buttered it, sprinkled the cinnamon sugar on top, passed it to my son, and went back to my sofa to sleep.

Several minutes later my son remarked, "This cinnamon is really spicy. It kind of burns my mouth."

I raised my head. "Maybe I got too much cinnamon in it this time."

"No," he said, "it tastes okay, it's just really hot."

Wearily I got up again, went over to the counter and looked at his plate. He'd already eaten one piece of toast. I picked up the remaining piece and sniffed it. It smelled like cinnamon. It looked like cinnamon. I took a bite and chewed. It tasted like cinnamon. For a moment. Then a searing heat penetrated the moist lining of my mouth. I swallowed. The after burn was intense.

"See what I mean?" he said. "You're trying to poison me, aren't you?"

I stared at him, perplexed, trying to figure out what I'd done.

"Maybe you put chili powder in by mistake," said my ex husband. "Here you are, worried about him getting killed on the highway and he's not even safe in his own kitchen."

"It's not chili powder," I said. "I don't know what it is."

Suddenly I had a sinking feeling. I went to the spice rack again and took out the cinnamon sugar. The bottle I usually used was an empty Paprika bottle with Paprika scribbled out and Cinnamon Sugar written in. But this wasn't the Paprika bottle. This bottle was labeled Cayenne.

MOM AND MACS

MacIntosh Apples are the only apples I'll eat. This has become more than a preference or tradition with me. It's become a dedication. A tribute to my mother.

Shortly after my four-year-old brother Wayne died of kidney disease, my father received a medical discharge from the Canadian Army and was subsequently laid off his job as a mechanic at Kelowna Motors. My mother had to go to work at a fruit packing house to support the family.

Each morning before the sun rose, while my sister and I were awake and getting ready for school, Dad would drive her to the Okanagan Packing Plant where she'd sort apples by hand and pack them into wooden crates to be shipped to grocers across the country.

When she'd been hired, the packing plant had issued Mom two pairs of silky white gloves with odd double fingertips to make it easier to sort the apples. These gloves fascinated me with their elegance, but though the double tips ruined their appearance, I could see no way to separate the layers and still retain the beauty of the glove. Besides, my mother needed them for work and reissued new ones would have to come out of her meager pay.

The Okanagan Valley of British Columbia produces an abundance and variety of fruit virtually unrivaled anywhere in the world. There are Bing cherries, Queen Anne cherries, Green Gage and Italian plums, Bartlett pears, Delicious apples of both the red and golden variety, and of course their most famous apple, the MacIntosh. We call them simply 'Macs'.

The skin of the MacIntosh is crisp and taut, unyielding at first to a bite, but then its flesh is sweet and soft. They make the best pies, juice and applesauce because they "fall" so perfectly when cooked. They taste the way apples are supposed to taste because their flavor has not been bred out of them in lieu of a more striking appearance. This is not to say that they aren't beautiful. They have a glorious bright red blush that covers three-quarters of the apple and often permeates the skin, turning the flesh pink. Then where the bright red leaves off, a soft pale green, the side not kissed by the sun, meets up. A perfect combination of sweet and tart.

Perks are few in a job like a packing plant, but the workers were allowed to take home apples that fell below market standards because of size, shape or appearance. These 'culls' were called 'juice apples', and employees could help themselves to a few. As my sister and I discovered, they were also 'pie apples,' for our mother's weary fingers could magically transform an uneven spotted half-dozen apples into the most delicious pie, a dish that often made up our entire dinner.

Mom worked at the packing plant for a least a year until Dad was able to find a job to support us, and my new baby brother came along. The hard repetitive work of grabbing and placing apples in boxes for ten hours a day resulted in her getting Carpal Tunnel Syndrome. My sister and I inherited the double finger-tipped gloves, which now held much less mystery for me than they had before.

When I left home I moved to another part of the country that bred and imported other types of apples, but not Macs. I was at a loss at how to bake a pie. What apples would 'fall' the way a Mac would when baked? Would they have enough juice, yet still allow the pie to hold its shape? Without answers to these dilemmas and not willing to experiment, I forsook cooking with apples for many years.

Then one day I saw them.

Even at a distance, without seeing the grocer's sign, I could tell their distinctive red and green skins. I walked over to the counter, picked up a Mac and smelled it. It smelled the way I remembered them from my childhood, unchanged by generations of orchardists who could have inadvertently ruined them, but managed not to.

I reached for a bag and as I placed the apples inside, my eyes filled with tears. I saw my mother's hands, once more in those weird double-fingertipped gloves, sorting thousands of apples a day for people just like me. People who will only eat Macs.

Apple Crisp

6 medium sized apples, MacIntosh preferred
1/4 cup granulated sugar
1 tsp cinnamon
1/4 cup butter
1/2 cup flour
3/4 cup brown sugar

Peel the apples and slice into a buttered baking dish. Mix sugar and cinnamon, sprinkle over apples. Combine the butter, brown sugar and flour, spread on top of apples. Bake at 350 F for 30 minutes or until apples are done and the top is browned.

Café au Lait Cake

2 1/2 cups sifted cake flour
1 2/3 cups granulated sugar
1 tsp salt
3/4 cup butter
3/4 cup milk
4 1/2 tsp baking powder
5 egg whites, unbeaten
1/4 cup milk
1/4 cup strong coffee (1/4 cup hot water and 2 heaping tsp instant coffee)
1 tsp vanilla

Heat oven to 375 F. Grease and flour 8 x 11" pan (or line 24 cupcake cups). Sift together into large electric mixer bowl, flour, sugar and salt. Drop in shortening, pour in 3/4 cup milk.

With mixer at low to medium speed, mix until all flour is dampened, then beat 2 minutes, scraping bowl and beaters as necessary. Stir in baking power, then add whites, remaining milk, 3 tbsp of coffee mix (reserve 1 tbsp for frosting), and vanilla. Beat 2 minutes longer. Bake 20 minutes or until done.

Coffee Frosting

1/4 cup butter
1 tsp vanilla
1 tbsp strong coffee mix (remainder from above)
2 cups powdered sugar

Beat all ingredients together until fluffy. Frost cake when cool.

Note: if you don't like the taste of coffee, substitute 1/2 cup milk less 2 tbsp in the second addition instead of 1/4 cup.

INDEX

Ambrosia Salad	Pg 27
Apple Crisp	Pg 116
Apple Pie	Pg 8
Asian Rice Salad	Pg 28
Baked Rum Bananas	Pg 38
Beef Wellington	Pg 61
Blender Croissants	Pg 59
Blueberry Pie	Pg 9
Brown Sugar Sauce	Pg 66
Butter Tarts	Pg 10
Cabbage Rolls	Pg 62
Café au Lait Cake	Pg 117
Caramel Popcorn	Pg 10
Carrot Cake	Pg 70
Carrot Pineapple Muffins	Pg 79
Chocolate Kiss Cookies	Pg 85
Chewy Chocolate Cookies	Pg 87
Chewy Pecan Cookies	Pg 86
Chicken Noodle Soup	Pg 35
Chicken Pie	Pg 47
Children's Playdough	Pg 99

Goodies from the Great White North

Cornish Pasties	Pg 49
Crazy Quilt Salad	Pg 29
Crustless Quiche Lorraine	Pg 58
Daiquiri Pie	Pg 11
Dill Dip	Pg 100
English Trifle	Pg 105
Fancy Whipped Shortbread	Pg 84
Finger Jello	Pg 99
Gazpacho	Pg 37
Gingersnaps	Pg 83
Gluhwein	Pg 22
Grasshopper Pie	Pg 13
Guacamole	Pg 100
Harvest Ribbon Cake	Pg 72
Hot Cabbage Salad	Pg 27
Hot Canadian Toddy	Pg 21
Indian Fry Bread	Pg 56
Lasagna	Pg 45
Lazy Daisy Cake	Pg 74
Licorice Caramels	Pg 94
Macaroons	Pg 88
Maple Pecan Squares	Pg 90
Marshmallow Dreams	Pg 75

Mocha Devil's Food Cake	Pg 16
Mulligatawny	Pg 36
Nanaimo Bars	Pg 92
Nutcracker Suite Cake	Pg 76
Oatmeal Raisin Cookies	Pg 80
Oh Henry Squares	Pg 91
Onions au Gratin	Pg 57
Party Punch	Pg 21
Pavlova	Pg 106
Perfect Pastry	Pg 7
Perogys	Pg 63
Pineapple Chicken	Pg 46
Shepherd's Pie	Pg 50
Strawberry Pie	Pg 14
Szechuan Beef	Pg 60
Tourtiere	Pg 65
Toy Chow Pie	Pg 15
Tropical Banana Bread	Pg 78
Unbaked Chocolate Cookies	Pg 89
Versatile Meat Sauce	Pg 44
Western Sandwiches	Pg 30

ABOUT THE AUTHOR

Leigh Goodison was born in Vancouver, Canada and moved to the U.S. in 1992. She is the author of *Renascence, Wild Ones, The Jigsaw Man* and *Limboland*, the first two books in the medical thriller series the St. Augustus Chronicles. She is also the author of *The Horse Trailer Owner's Manual*. Her articles, essays, short stories and poetry have appeared in publications across North America. She currently lives in Washington state.

www.ingramcontent.com/pod-product-compliance
Lightning Source LLC
Chambersburg PA
CBHW021154080526
44588CB00008B/333